FRU[IT]
BERRY
GARDENING
for CANADA

© 2009 by Lone Pine Publishing
First printed in 2009 10 9 8 7 6 5 4 3 2 1
Printed in Canada

The Publisher: Lone Pine Publishing
10145 – 81 Avenue
Edmonton, AB T6E 1W9
Canada
Website: www.lonepinepublishing.com

Library and Archives Canada Cataloguing in Publication

Donnelly, Louise, 1953-
   Fruit and berry gardening for Canada / Louise Donnelly, Alison Beck.

Includes index.
ISBN 978-1-55105-620-3

   1. Fruit-culture--Canada. I. Beck, Alison, 1971- II. Title.

SB357.D65 2009   634.0971   C2008-907796-2

Editorial Director: Nancy Foulds
Editorial: Sheila Quinlan, Nicholle Carriere
Photo Coordinator: Don Williamson
Production Manager: Gene Longson
Book Design, Layout & Production: Rob Tao
Cover Design: Gerry Dotto

All photos by Tim Matheson and Nanette Samol, except: Janet Davis 195b; Joan de Grey 101a, 215; Don Doucette 127b; Tamara Eder 29, 38a&b, 41abcde&f, 44, 46a&b, 47, 68a, 69a, 72, 73, 80, 103a, 105a, 119a, 127a, 137b, 147b, 190, 191a&b; Elliot Engley 35, 36a&b, 37, 39; Jen Fafard 136; Derek Fell 10, 14, 15a&b, 16, 24, 25, 28, 49, 84, 85b, 86, 87a, 88a&b, 89a, 90, 91, 96, 97a, 98b, 101b, 104, 110, 111a&b, 112a, 113a&b, 115a, 116a, 117a, 128a&b, 138, 142, 143a, 144b, 146, 148, 149b, 152, 153a, 156a, 157, 158, 161a, 162b, 164, 165, 166, 167a&b, 172, 176b, 178b, 180, 183a&b, 184, 185a, 197b, 198b, 199a, 207, 208, 209a&b, 211a&b, 214; Ann Gordon 92; Saxon Holt 23, 112b, 122, 144a, 149a, 159, 173, 181b, 182; Liz Klose 71; Olga Langerova 185b; L. Lauzuma 186; Heather Markham 205a; Marilynn McAra 121a; Steve Nikkila 192, 193a, 194; Allison Penko 119b, 130, 170b, 181a, 204a&b; Laura Peters 18, 22a, 33, 60, 137a, 153a, 170a, 189, 197a, 199b, 201; Photos.com 210; Robert Ritchie 68b, 108, 135b, 203b, 76, 77; Mark Turner 147a, 179b; Sandy Weatherall half-title, title, 82100, 125, 134, 196; Don Williamson 124, 139a&b; Carol Woo 66a; Tim Wood 109a&b, 169b, 177a, 178a, 193b.

All illustrations by Ian Sheldon.

The frost free days map (p. 26) and the hardiness zones map (p. 27) were adapted from *The Atlas of Canada* (http://atlas.gc.ca) © 2008. Produced under licince from Her Majesty the Queen in Right of Canada, with permission of Natural Resources Canada.

We acknowledge the financial support of the Government of Canada through the Book Publishing Industry Development Program (BPIDP) for our publishing activities.

PC: 1

FRUIT & BERRY GARDENING for CANADA

Louise Donnelly
Alison Beck

Lone Pine Publishing

CONTENTS

Almond•Apricot
p. 84

Apple
p. 86

Bayberry
p. 92

Beech
p. 94

Banana
p. 90

Blueberry•Cranberry•Huckleberry
p. 96

Cape Gooseberry
p. 100

Chestnut
p. 106

Chokeberry
p. 108

Citrus
p. 110

Cherry
p. 102

Currant•Gooseberry
p. 114

Elderberry
p. 118

Fig
p. 120

Ginkgo
p. 122

Goji Berry
p. 124

Grape
p. 126

Hawthorn
p. 130

Hazelnut
p. 134

Highbush Cranberry
p. 136

Juniper Berry
p. 138

Kiwi
p. 140

Melon
p. 142

Mulberry
p. 146

Olive
p. 148

Oregon Grapeholly
p. 150

Passionfruit
p. 152

Peach·Nectarine
p. 154

Peanut
p. 158

Pear
p. 160

Pecan·Hickory
p. 164

Persimmon
p. 166

Plum
p. 174

Pine Nut
p. 168

Pineapple
p. 172

Prickly Pear
p. 180

Raspberry•Blackberry
p. 184

Rhubarb
p. 188

Quince
p. 182

Rosehip
p. 190

Serviceberry
p. 192

Squash
p. 196

Walnut
p. 206

Watermelon
p. 210

Strawberry
p. 200

Sumac
p. 202

Wintergreen
p. 212

Introduction

For many of us, our garden is a small backyard vegetable patch, with a sampler of tidy (or not so tidy) rows of carrots and beans and a hill or two of cucumbers alongside. Maybe a few tomato plants and some parsley or basil. The odd year we might squeeze in a little corn or an unusual hot pepper. Or perhaps our garden is a flowerbed, stocked with reliable perennials and a few annuals added for their dash of season-long colour. We might even have both, enjoying delicious fresh vegetables and attractive flowers. But what about fruit?

Fruit is grown in Canada on a commercial basis in pockets across the country where temperatures generally do not go much lower than -20° C: mainly areas in the Maritime provinces, southern Ontario and British Columbia. On the prairies, university researchers have for decades produced high-quality, hardy fruits including apples and cherries.

A home gardener might be initially hesitant to give fruit a try. However, if one year you successfully raised pumpkins, you were already growing fruit! Those orange globes are actually the edible fruit of the trailing varieties of two members of the gourd family. Do you have a rugosa rose or two in the garden? Or a prickly but handsome Oregon grapeholly? Again, you've been growing fruit. The swollen pod, or "hip," left after the rose petals have fallen is rich in vitamin C and makes a nutritious tea or an elegant jelly.

The clusters of indigo grapeholly berries also make a fine jelly or a tart, refreshing juice.

Perhaps, though, rosehips and grapeholly berries aren't your idea of homegrown fruit. What about peaches and cherries? Lemons? Walnuts and chestnuts? Figs, kiwis or trendy goji berries?

Often with no more effort than it takes to raise tomatoes or cultivate roses, you can grow your own fruit. Even a small effort will readily supplement your store-bought supply of fruit. Don't let lack of space or time deter you. Many species of fruit take up only a small area and are low maintenance. And you don't necessarily need a greenhouse. In fact, Canada's temperate climate is ideal for growing many fruits. Apples and currants, for example, require frost and cold winters for good fruit production.

Depending on your hardiness zone, you might not be able to grow all the fruit covered in this book. And you may not be inclined to nurse a passionflower or a prickly pear to the fruiting stage or to wait for a slow-growing nut tree to bear fruit. Or maybe you don't want to struggle with olive trees and figs and their demands for mild winters and sheltered sites. But no matter where you live or how little patience you have for finicky gardening, there are fruits that you can grow and harvest in your backyard or on a patio or balcony.

Grapes

Why Grow Fruit?

Taste

There are many compelling reasons to grow your own fruit. First and foremost is simply taste. Just like biting into a sun-warmed cherry tomato (which, botanically speaking, is a fruit but is more often regarded and treated as a vegetable), the flavour of freshly picked raspberries is sublime. Peaches and other stone fruits are much tastier if you can wait for them to ripen on the tree rather than picking them green to withstand shipping and the potential of rough handling in the supermarket. Rhubarb is sweeter; grapes are less bruised.

AVAILABILITY

When you harvest your own fruit you control not only the quality, but also the availability. If you wake up one morning hungering for rhubarb muffins, the main ingredient is just steps from the kitchen. You can head out in pyjamas, pull a half-dozen green and ruby stalks, and have the muffins in the oven before the coffee's even ready. Need an elegant dessert in a hurry? Crown fresh raspberries with a dollop of rich yogourt, a sprinkle of brown sugar and a sprig of mint. Served with panache, no one will ever know how little effort it took.

Yet attempting to buy those raspberries might be an entirely different story. Fresh raspberries are notoriously difficult to ship. Even transported in tiny baskets, they are easily crushed by their own weight. In no time at all, luscious, perfect berries can be reduced to a juicy mess. Local farm markets and direct sales are a better bet, but they sell out quickly. Avid jam makers snap up 10-kilo flats, and single baskets disappear as fast as the vendors put them out. If you are lucky enough to snag a basket or two, the price could well give you pause.

COST

Seasonal delights such as fresh berries fetch a premium return. It's not only that they're in demand, but also that they're fiddly to harvest. Hand picking, careful packaging and transportation all add to the cost. Often much of the purchase price of fruit is to cover labour-intensive production and shipping.

Currants

Environmental and Health Rewards

Besides the financial savings, when you produce your own fruit, you control the growing conditions. You decide the ratio of chemical to organic fertilizer and pest control, how much water to use, and how the fruit is harvested and stored. And that brings us to health benefits.

Homegrown fruits are fresher and, as a result, more nutrient-dense. Grown at home, fruits don't have to endure long shipping, poor storage or less-than-ideal cultivation practices. Fruit, which includes nuts, provides vitamins, calcium, protein, fibre and good fat, and aids in the absorption of iron. If growing fruit simply means you have more on hand to consume or your interest in fruit and a healthy diet is piqued, that's all to the good.

Gooseberries

Versatility

Fruit adapts well to both sweet and savoury dishes. Apple pie springs readily to mind, but apples make a tasty addition to turkey stuffing or, lightly sautéed in a dab of butter with a dusting of freshly chopped rosemary, to pork roast. In Asian cuisine, pumpkin is more likely to be served in a stew than a pie. It also makes a terrific cold-weather soup. For a refreshing summer soup, blend puréed plums with buttermilk or crème fraîche. Or simultaneously pour chilled cantaloupe and honeydew melon purée enlivened with lime juice into opposite sides of a small, flat soup bowl to create an enchanting bicoloured presentation.

Easy Storage

If you're overwhelmed with an abundant harvest, fruit is easy to store. Few of us will likely have the cool, humid cellar recommended for long-term storage of fresh grapes (laid on trays, they'll keep for months), but they can be frozen individually or in small clusters on cookie sheets and then bagged for the freezer. Berries store well this way, too, and can be brought out at your leisure and made into jams or used for desserts or, slightly thawed, simply eaten as they are. Apples do well in a garage, boxed and covered with a sleeping bag or two, as long as the temperature remains above freezing. Nuts are small and don't take up much pantry storage. Pumpkins will often last the winter in a cool, dry basement. Even a little extra space in the fridge will extend the time you can enjoy homegrown fruit.

More Choice

Growing your own fruit lets you choose the variety. Commercial orchards and farms tend to grow a particular fruit for its shipping qualities or colour and looks (as opposed to taste). The home gardener can grow strictly for flavour without having to worry if the fruit has an appealing and marketable appearance. A pretty face doesn't always guarantee an equally attractive taste. The home gardener can also take risks a commercial grower can't afford and attempt iffy crops such as peanuts or figs.

Preservation and Tradition

There's also an opportunity to reintroduce and preserve our vanishing heritage varieties or to leave a living legacy. Many nut and fruit trees will outlast the gardener who planted them. Rhubarb plants and raspberry canes can be passed along to friends and family, ensuring a bit of your garden carries on in theirs.

The Best for Last

A final, and possibly the best, reason to grow your own fruit is simply for the satisfaction and pleasure and fun all gardens so generously provide. Gardens bring families and generations together. Remember patting the soil around a strawberry plant with your grandfather? Or lifting a child to pluck a rosy apple? A garden just as easily provides solitude and time to think. It gives us exercise and fresh air. It sustains, nourishes and challenges. The harvest, as the old saying goes, is just the cherry on the cake.

Peaches (above), pear (below)

Types of Fruit

*F*ruit, as noted, is as diverse as pumpkin and fig. It can be the common apple or the exotic passionfruit. Here are some loose categories to consider.

Annual Fruits

Annual fruits grow from seed, produce flowers that develop into fruit and then die, all in one growing season. Examples are peanut, squash and melon. Sometimes, tender perennials, which don't survive our Canadian winters, are treated as annuals and grown accordingly.

Perennial Fruits

Perennials are any plants that last more than two years and usually flower—and fruit—annually. Non-woody perennial fruits include strawberry, wintergreen and, though technically a vegetable, rhubarb.

Tree, Shrub and Vine Fruits

Trees, such as peach and chestnut, are woody plants that grow from a single stem. Shrubs, such as blueberry and rose, grow from a group, or cluster, of woody stems. Vines, such as kiwi and grape, have slender woody stems and do not stand by themselves, but instead crawl along the ground or twine themselves up a support. Several types of fruit are borne on these woody plants.

BERRIES

Berries are any small, juicy fruits with seeds rather than pits. This category includes a large number of plants, such as serviceberry, currant and grape. One advantage of choosing berries is that the plants bear fruit much sooner than trees, often in the second year, and take up less space than even a dwarf tree.

DRUPES

Drupes are any fruits with a thin skin covering soft flesh and a hard pit or stone at the fruit's centre that contains one or a few seeds. Examples are apricot, olive and plum.

NUTS

Nuts are fruits with a hard, woody shell surrounding an edible kernel. Nuts include walnut, pecan and, for the purposes of this book, pine nuts, though a pine nut is actually a seed.

POMES

Pomes, such as apple, pear and quince, have firm, juicy flesh surrounding a seedy core.

EXOTIC/TROPICAL FRUITS

These tender, non-native fruits, such as banana, pineapple and passionfruit, need coddling and do not survive our Canadian winters without indoor protection. They are most often grown as novelties.

Pine nuts (above), rhubarb (below)

WORKING FRUIT INTO THE GARDEN

*I*f you've got the space and energy, certainly consider a small orchard or vineyard or several rows of raspberries, strawberries and other berries. As we mentioned, storing the harvested bounty is not difficult, and family and friends will always line up for a share of fresh, homegrown fruit. Most of us, though, will likely want to start small and incorporate a few fruits into our existing gardens.

You don't have to plant a whole apple orchard or set aside large areas for strawberries or grapes. Fruiting plants suit both kitchen gardens and ornamental beds and are easily incorporated into existing gardens or landscaping. You might be doing that now with a few strawberries edging the vegetables or an elegant old apple tree gracing the front yard.

Strawberry plants are a good start and can easily be worked into the vegetable garden. Mulch them well to keep the berries clean, and keep an eye on the runners, which quickly sprout "babies." An old gardener's advice for the first year is to tuck two baby plants in close to the mother plant and completely snip away all other runners.

With their attractive foliage (the green leaves turn a lovely red in autumn) and pretty flowers, strawberries also look right at home edging the flowerbed. They do well in containers and are a natural for window boxes, hanging baskets or planters. Garden centres often carry terracotta and other types of pots specifically designed for raising strawberries. Other fruits and specific varieties suitable for container growing are covered in this book.

Shrubs or bushes, such as the aromatic black currant, can hold their own as a decorative plant in the flowerbed as long as you give a little thought to their placement. You'll want room to stay on top of the pruning, the weeding out of unwanted suckers and the eventual berry harvest. You'll also want to avoid planting where falling berries can stain walkways or be easily tracked into the house. Site shrubs and bushes with the same thought you'd give to long-lived and seldom-moved perennials.

If you're planning a hedge, rather than the ubiquitous cedar or privet, consider rugosa roses. Their dense and spiny growth is a deterrent to humans and beasts alike with the plus of gorgeous, fragrant blooms and colourful and nutritious hips. Raspberries and other fruit-bearing canes also make a rustic and edible hedge.

Fruit and nut trees add a distinctive note to the landscape, and many dwarf or mid-size varieties are available for the home garden. On the other hand, a single specimen or a pair (if necessary for good fruiting) of tall, stately, nut-bearing trees can serve as the focal point for all your landscaping plans as well as providing abundant shade in summer.

Currants

Many fruit-bearing trees and shrubs lend themselves to pruning to control their size. Pears and apples have a long history of espalier. Derived from the French *epaulet*, meaning a shoulder strap and referring to the way limbs branch, shoulder-like, at a right angle to the trunk, espaliered trees are trained to grow against a wall. With judicious and severe pruning, the tree grows only in two directions—in height (but pruning controls that as well) and flat along the wall. Espalier allows for fruit trees in narrow sites, such as along a walkway or in a walled courtyard or surrounding a patio. The trees can also be trained along free-standing trellises or horizontal wires.

Citrus, which for just about all of Canada will be container grown and brought indoors over winter, can still grow quite large. Again, pruning will keep the plant a manageable size. Pruning can also be employed to increase production in many fruit plants, maximizing the return for the space they take up.

Crabapple

GARDENING ENVIRONMENT

*A*lthough it may not be as much fun as a whirlwind trip through the plant nursery, it's a good idea, before selecting a single plant, to take stock of your garden and its environment first. Rather than attempting to make your growing conditions suit your choice of fruit, it's much easier and more productive to match the plant to your garden. Plants grown in their preferred conditions tend to thrive. They're healthier and less prone to pest and disease problems, and yields are often more generous. It might help to sketch out your garden on graph paper, noting garden and structure orientation (north, south, etc.), shaded and sunny spots, exposed areas susceptible to wind, low-lying areas susceptible to frost, and so forth. Study your garden's light levels, soil types and exposure, such as to wind, sun, frost and salt spray, and know your hardiness zone and frost dates.

Oregon grapeholly

Squash (above), grapes (below)

Light

The four basic categories of light are full sun, partial shade, light shade and full shade. Buildings, fences, other trees and even the time of year will influence how much light your garden gets. Full sun areas, such as a south-facing wall, receive sunlight all or most of the day. A partial shade location, such as an east- or west-facing wall, is sunny part of the day and shady part of the day. Light shade locations are in shade most or all of the day, but some light gets through to ground level. The area

under a small-leaved tree is often lightly shaded. Full shade areas, such as the north side of a building, receive no direct sunlight at all.

Depending where you live, full sun can be more intense than for other areas of the country. Full sun in the hot Okanagan Valley in the interior of British Columbia, for example, is much stronger than on the cooler coast.

In general, fruit plants need sunlight—lots of it. Although some fruits, such as the apple, might require cool autumn nights for good colour and flavour, a long, warm growing season with plenty of sunlight is essential for a successful crop.

Soil

Soil holds air, water, nutrients and organic matter, all vital to healthy plants. Sandy soil drains quickly, and nutrients are washed away. It also contains lots of air and doesn't compact easily. Clay soil holds water well, drains slowly and holds most nutrients, but there is little room for air, and clay compacts easily. A soil with a mix of sand and clay is called loam.

How quickly your soil drains is a consideration when planning what to grow. A rocky hillside garden will lose water quickly, while a low-lying area could remain moist and boggy. Water retention in sandy soil can be improved with the addition of organic matter, while drainage can

Peanuts

be encouraged in wet areas by adding sand or gravel to the soil. Building raised beds can also improve drainage.

The acidity or alkalinity of the soil influences the availability of nutrients and is another aspect to consider when deciding which types of fruit to grow. The scale on which acidity or alkalinity is rated is called the pH scale, which ranges from 0 to 14. Soil with a pH lower than 7 is considered acidic; soil with a pH higher than 7 is considered alkaline. In general, fruit plants do best with soils that are slightly acidic to neutral (a pH of 6.5 to 7). A few fruits, such as blueberries, prefer a more acidic soil. Soil-testing kits are available at garden centres.

EXPOSURE

Blistering sun, harsh winds, salt spray and frost pockets all take a toll on the success of the garden and the eventual harvest. Take a good look at your garden. What sort of exposure do you have? Does the wind tear through your yard? Are there low-lying frost pockets? Are there sheltered areas? Do some areas get more sun than others? Your garden is exposed to wind, heat, cold and rain, and some plants are better adapted than others to withstand these forces. Whenever possible, select a sunny yet protected spot for your fruiting plants. Often a sheltered area allows you to push the boundaries of your hardiness zone and makes it possible to harvest fruit that you might otherwise not be able to grow.

Melons

Wind and heat are the most likely elements to damage your fruiting plants, and cold can affect their survival. The sun can be very intense, and heat can rise quickly on a sunny afternoon, so only use plants that tolerate or even thrive in hot weather in the hot spots in your garden. Plants can become dehydrated in windy locations, and strong winds can knock over tall, stiff-stemmed plants. Plants that do not require staking in a sheltered location may need support in one that is more exposed. Temper the effect of the wind with hedges or trees. A solid wall creates wind turbulence on the downwind side, but a looser structure, such as a hedge, breaks up the force and protects a larger area.

Rain—too much or too heavy—can damage some plants. Most will recover, but some are slow to do so. Grow-covers—light fabric supported by wire—allow sun, air and moisture in and keep bugs, birds and wet weather out. For exposed sites, choose plants or varieties that are quick to recover from rain damage.

Persimmons

Frost Dates and Hardiness Zones

Gardening conditions differ dramatically from the relatively balmy but damp weather of the southern portion of Canada's west coast to the temperamental coastal storms of the east coast. Northern gardens, while blessed with plenty of hours of daylight, are hampered by a short growing season and the dangers of a late frost in spring or an early frost in autumn. The fertile prairies go from extremely hot in summer to bitterly cold in winter. The best bet for growing fruit is to choose plants suited to your geographical area.

All gardeners need to be aware of frost dates and hardiness zones. Last-frost and first-frost dates vary greatly from year to year and region to region, as do minimum winter temperatures, but the averages for your region will help you choose fruits that will survive in your garden. Consult your local garden centre for more specific information. Perennials should be hardy enough to survive winter outdoors, and annuals will need the right conditions to grow to a mature size in a single season.

Annuals are grouped into categories based on cold-weather tolerance:

FROST FREE DAYS MAP

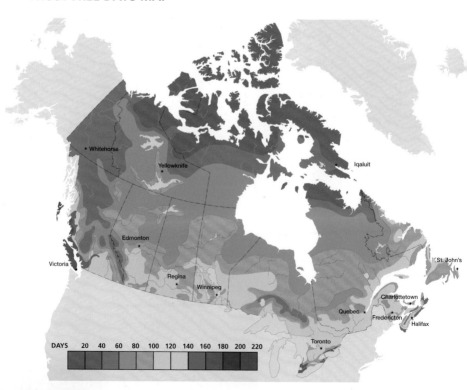

hardy, semi-hardy and tender. Hardy annuals tolerate low temperatures and even frost. Many hardy annuals can be seeded directly into the garden before the last spring frost date. Semi-hardy annuals tolerate a light frost but will be killed by a heavy one. These annuals can be planted around the last-frost date and will generally benefit from being started early from seed indoors, just like transplants from garden centres. Tender annuals have no frost tolerance at all and might suffer if the temperature drops to even just a few degrees above freezing. These plants are often started early indoors and are not planted in the garden until the last-frost date has passed and the ground has had a chance to warm up. Some have the advantage of tolerating hot summer temperatures.

When it comes to perennials, including trees and shrubs, gardeners need to know their hardiness zone. The hardiness zone map is based on average minimum winter temperatures and plant survival data. Many plants also have a maximum temperature threshold, above which they may die. Canada has a wide range of hardiness zones. Check the map to find yours.

HARDINESS ZONES MAP

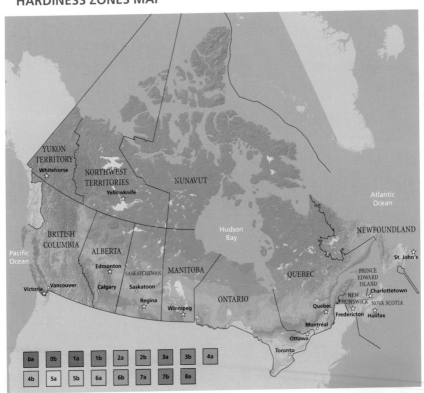

Perennials are given a hardiness zone designation, but don't feel intimidated or limited by this information. Mild or harsh winters, heavy or light snow cover, autumn care and the overall health of your plants all influence their ability to survive through winter.

In addition, local garden topography creates microclimates—small areas more or less favourable for growing plants that are out of zone in the rest of your garden. Microclimates may be created, for example, in the shelter of a nearby building or a stand of evergreen trees, in a hollow or at the top of a windswept hill, or near a large body of water. Microclimates can raise the zone a notch and allow you the possibility of growing a type of fruit that everyone says won't thrive in your particular area. Experimenting with plants that are borderline hardy is a challenging and fun part of gardening.

Lemons

PREPARING THE GARDEN

*T*aking the time before you start planting to properly prepare the garden beds will save you time and effort later on in summer. Loosen the soil with a large garden fork and remove all the weeds. Amending the soil with organic matter prior to planting is the first step in caring for your plants. Avoid working the soil when it is very wet or very dry because you will damage the soil structure by breaking down the pockets that hold air and water.

All soils, from the heaviest clay to the lightest sand, benefit from the addition of organic matter because it adds nutrients as well as improves the soil structure. Organic matter improves heavy clay soils by loosening them and allowing air and water to penetrate, and it improves sandy or light soils by increasing the ability of the soils to retain water, which allows plants to absorb nutrients before they are leached away. Common organic additives for your soil are grass clippings, shredded leaves, peat moss, chopped straw or well-rotted manure. Mix organic matter into the soil with a garden fork. Within a few months, earthworms and other decomposer organisms will break down the organic matter; at the same time, their activities will keep the soil from compacting.

Espalier pear

Composting materials

Compost can be purchased from most garden centres, but making it yourself is a relatively simple process. Compost can be made in a pile, a wooden box or a purchased composter. Kitchen scraps, grass clippings and autumn leaves will eventually break down if simply left alone. The process can be sped up if a few simple guidelines are followed.

Use brown (dry) as well as green (fresh) materials with a higher proportion of brown to green matter. Brown matter includes chopped straw, shredded leaves or sawdust, and green matter may be vegetable scraps, grass clippings or pulled weeds. Green matter breaks down quickly and produces nitrogen, which feeds decomposer organisms while they break down brown matter.

COMPOST

Any organic matter you add will be of greater benefit to your soil if it has been composted first. In forests, meadows or other natural environments, organic debris such as leaves and various plant bits break down on the soil surface, and the nutrients are gradually made available to the plants that are growing there. In the home garden, where pests and diseases may be a problem and where untidy debris isn't practical, a compost pile or bin creates a controlled environment where organic matter can be fully broken down before being introduced to your garden. Compost is a great regular additive for your fruit garden, and good composting methods will help reduce pest and disease problems.

Egg shells, coffee grounds and filters, tea bags and lint from your vacuum cleaner and dryer are all beneficial additions, but do not add dog or cat feces, kitty litter, fats, dairy or meat to the mix. These items will attract pests and will begin to smell, resulting in a mess. Do not put diseased or pest-ridden material into your compost pile—you risk spreading problems throughout your entire garden. If you do put questionable material in the pile, put it as near the centre as possible, where the temperatures are highest.

Spread the green materials evenly throughout the pile by layering them between brown materials. Layers of soil or finished compost will introduce the organisms necessary to

FOOD WASTE DONOR

Please put your food waste
in blue bins. Do not feed
compost bins directly. T...
...se bags and contain...
wash with you...

GREENWASTE

...se put any materials
...e grass, plants and
...den waste in adjacent
storage area.

YES	NO
• uncooked fruit and vegetable waste • egg shells • coffee grounds and filters • tea bags	• meat, fish, poultry, cooked food • grains (bread, bagels, pasta, rice, perogies, etc.) • dairy products • fats, oils • really wet, smelly food waste • twist ties, elastic bands

Wooden compost bins

break down the organic matter properly. If the pile seems very dry, add a bit of water as you layer. The pile needs to be moist but not soggy. Adding nitrogen, such as that found in fertilizer, can help speed up the composting process, but avoid strong concentrations that can kill beneficial organisms.

The pile can be left to sit and will eventually be ready to use if you are willing to wait several months to a year. To speed up decomposition, aerate the material by turning the pile over or poking holes into it with a pitchfork every week or two. A well-aerated compost pile will generate a lot of heat. Use a thermometer attached to a long probe, like a giant meat thermometer, to take the temperature near the middle of the

pile. Compost can easily reach 71° C (160° F) while decomposing. This heat will destroy weed seeds and kill many damaging soil organisms. Most beneficial organisms are not killed unless the temperature rises above 71° C. Once your compost pile reaches 71° C, let it sit. If you notice the temperature dropping significantly, turn the pile to aerate it, stimulating the process to start again.

Your compost has reached the end of its cycle when you can no longer recognize the matter that went into it and when the temperature no longer rises when you turn the pile. It may take as little as one month to reach this stage, at which time the compost, rich in nutrients and beneficial organisms, is ready to be spread onto your garden.

Plastic composting bins (above), composting worms (below)

If you have limited space, you can still make compost using redworms, available at any bait shop. Worm composting, also known as vermicomposting, takes up little room and requires little of your time and resources. Many municipalities offer courses in worm composting, and there are also resources online or at your local library or bookstore. In as little as six weeks, the worms will create usable, nutrient-rich compost.

SELECTING FRUITING PLANTS

Fruiting plants can be purchased or acquired as seeds, cuttings, bare roots, balled-and-burlapped stock or potted plants. The type of fruit you choose to grow will determine whether you should begin with seeds or with a more mature form of the plant. Some annuals, peanuts for example, are relatively easy to start from seed. Some varieties of strawberries also can be grown from seed, but it's much easier to start with a plant. Bramble fruits, such as raspberry shrubs, can be grown from canes. Canes, or suckers, grow from underground stems or roots.

If you plan on growing fruit and nut trees, these are sold as bare-root, balled-and-burlapped or container stock. Bare-root stock has roots surrounded with moist sawdust or peat moss and a plastic wrapping. Often sold through mail-order companies, it's the least expensive choice. Stock should be kept moist and cool and planted as soon as possible in spring.

Balled-and-burlapped (B&B) stock comes with the roots surrounded by soil and wrapped in burlap; often a wire cage further secures larger plants. The plants are usually field grown, dug up, balled and burlapped the year they are sold. B&B stock is less expensive than container stock, but often, many of the roots have been severed, necessitating extra care after transplanting. B&B stock can be planted any time during the growing season.

Container stock is grown in pots filled with potting soil and has established roots. It is the most expensive option and reflects the months or years put into raising the plant. Container stock is easy to transplant, is easily established and can be planted any time during the growing season.

Typical garden centre

Choosing Healthy Plants

Never purchase a weak, damaged or unhealthy looking plant or root. Even if it costs less, it's unlikely to mature into a vigorous plant capable of producing harvestable fruit. Look at freebies in the same light. Being selective at the start will pay off down the road.

Plants should be compact and have good colour. Tall, leggy plants have been deprived of light. If a potted plant has leaves that appear to be chewed or damaged, inspect for insects. Examine leaf and flower buds. If they are dry and fall off easily, the plant has been deprived of necessary moisture. Stems should be strong, supple and unbroken. Shrubs should be bushy, and trees should have a strong leader (the leader is the shoot growing from the main branch). Avoid trees and shrubs with bark damage.

Check the roots of any plants you want to purchase. Root balls should be soft and moist. Do not buy plants with dry root balls. Also pass up any container stock that has roots encircling the inside of the pot. A root-bound plant, especially a tree, will not do well.

The plant on the right is much healthier than the plant on the left

PLANTING FRUITING PLANTS

STARTING SEEDS INDOORS

Many desirable fruits need a longer growing season than most of Canada provides. Plants such as melons that do not tolerate frost and cold are easiest to grow when they are purchased as bedding plants in spring and then planted out when the soil is warm and all danger of frost has passed. However, if you want to grow an unusual variety of melon, or any other warm-weather fruit, you may have to order seeds from a specialty catalogue and start them indoors.

Seeds can be started in pots or, if you need a lot of plants, flats. Use a sterile soil mix intended for starting seeds. The soil will generally need to be kept moist but not soggy. Most seeds germinate in moderately warm temperatures of about 14°–21° C (57°–70° F).

Many seed-starting supplies are available at garden centres. Some are useful, but many are not necessary. Seed-tray dividers are useful. The dividers, often called plug trays, are made of plastic and prevent seedling roots from tangling together and from being disturbed when the seedlings are transplanted. Heating coils or pads can also be useful. Placed under the pots or flats, they keep the soil at a constant temperature.

Basic materials for starting seeds

Use a folded piece of paper to handle tiny seeds

All seedlings are susceptible to damping off. Damping off occurs when a fungus causes an apparently healthy seedling to topple over and die. Close inspection will reveal a blackened, pinched area at soil level. Sterile soil mix, good air circulation and evenly moist soil will help prevent this problem. Products to prevent damping off are also available at your local garden centre.

Once you have your supplies, fill your pot or seed tray with the soil mix and press it down slightly—not too firmly, or the soil will not drain. Wet the soil before planting your seeds, or they may wash into clumps if the soil is watered after the seeds are planted. Large seeds can be planted individually and spaced out in pots or trays. If you have divided inserts for your trays, plant one or two seeds per section. Small seeds may have to be sprinkled over the soil mix a bit more randomly. Fold a sheet of paper in half and place the small seeds in the crease. Gently tap the underside of the fold to bounce or roll the seeds off the paper in a more controlled manner. Some seeds are so tiny that they look like dust. These seeds can be mixed with a small quantity of fine sand and spread on the soil surface. These tiny seeds will not need to be covered with any more soil. Medium-sized seeds can be lightly covered, and

A mister allows gentle watering

A cover on the seed tray helps keep in moisture

large seeds can be pressed into the soil and then lightly covered. Do not cover seeds that need to be exposed to light to germinate. Water using a very fine spray if the soil starts to dry out. A hand-held spray bottle will moisten the soil without disturbing the seeds.

Plant only one type of seed in each pot or flat. Each species has a different rate of germination, and the germinated seedlings will require different conditions than the seeds that have yet to germinate. To keep the environment moist, place the pot inside a clear plastic bag. Change the bag or turn it inside out once condensation starts to build up and drip. The plastic bag can be held up with stakes or wires poked in around the edges of the pot. Many seed trays come with clear plastic covers that can be placed over the flats to keep the moisture in. Remove the covers once the seeds have germinated.

Seeds generally don't need a lot of light to germinate, so pots or trays can be kept in a warm, out-of-the-way place. Once the seeds have germinated, place them in a bright location but out of direct sun. Transplant seedlings to individual pots once they have three or four true leaves. (True leaves look like mature leaves; the first one or two leaves are actually part of the seed.) Plants in trays can be left until neighbouring leaves start to touch each other. At this point, the plants will be competing for light and should be transplanted to individual pots.

Do not fertilize young seedlings. Fertilizer will cause seedlings to produce soft, spindly growth that is susceptible to attack by insects and diseases. The seed itself provides all the nutrition the seedling needs. A fertilizer, diluted to quarter- or half-strength, can be used once seedlings have four or five true leaves.

Planting Outside

Specific growing advice is listed with each individual fruit covered in this guide. Here, though, are some general guidelines.

Plant as early in the growing season as the weather allows. Many plants, such as strawberries, will take a light frost. For more tender plants such as melons, wait until all danger of frost is past and the soil is warm. Plant seeds at the recommended depth. More detailed information is given below for planting potted plants or seedlings as well as trees and shrubs.

POTTED PLANTS AND SEEDLINGS

Start by digging a hole about twice the width of the pot or seed-tray plug. Remove the plant from the pot or seed tray. If the pot is small enough, you can hold your hand across the top of the pot, letting your fingers straddle the stem of the plant, and then turn it upside down. Never pull on the stem or leaves to get a plant out of a pot. It is better to cut a difficult pot off rather than risk damaging the plant. To prevent the roots from drying out, do not unpot the plants until immediately before you transplant.

Gently spread out the roots as you plant, teasing a few roots out of the soil ball to get the plant growing in the right direction. If the roots have become densely wound around the inside of the pot, cut into or score the root mass with a sharp knife to encourage new growth into the surrounding soil. If there is a solid mat at the bottom of the root ball, remove it. Such roots will not be able to spread out and establish themselves in the soil; the new root tips will only become trapped in the existing mass.

Place the plant in the prepared hole. It should be planted at the same level that it was at in the pot, or a little higher, to allow for the soil to settle. If the plant is too low in the ground, it may rot when rain collects around the crown. Fill the soil in around the roots and firm it down. Water the plant well as soon as you have planted it and regularly until it has become established.

Sizing up the hole

Digging the hole

Root-bound plant

PLANTING BARE-ROOT STOCK

Remove any plastic or sawdust from the roots. Soak the entire root system of bare-root trees and shrubs in a bucket of water for 12 hours prior to planting. When planting shrubs or trees, dig a generous-sized hole. The hole for bare-root stock should be large enough to accommodate the expanded roots with a little extra room to spare. The centre of the hole should be deep enough so that soil will just cover the roots. Increase the depth of the hole around the edges. This hole shape prevents the plant from sinking as the soil settles and encourages excess water to drain away from the new plant. Centre the plant in the hole and backfill slowly, settling the soil with water as you go.

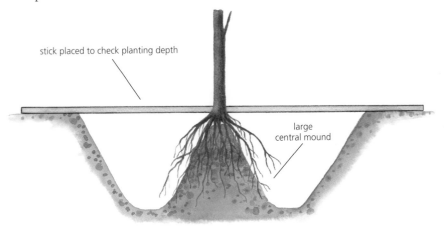

stick placed to check planting depth

large
central mound

Planting bare-root stock

PLANTING BALLED-AND-BURLAPPED STOCK

For balled-and-burlapped trees and shrubs, the diameter of the hole should be about twice the width of the root ball. It is always best to remove any burlap from around the root ball to prevent girdling and to maximize contact between the roots and the soil. If roots are already growing through the burlap, remove as much burlap as you can while avoiding damage to these new roots.

If a wire basket holds the burlap in place, it should be removed as well.

With the basket removed, set the still-burlapped plant on the centre mound in the hole. Lean the plant over to one side and roll the upper part of the burlap down to the ground. When you lean the plant in the opposite direction, you can often pull the burlap out from under the roots. If the tree is difficult to move once in the hole, you may need to cut away as much burlap as you can instead.

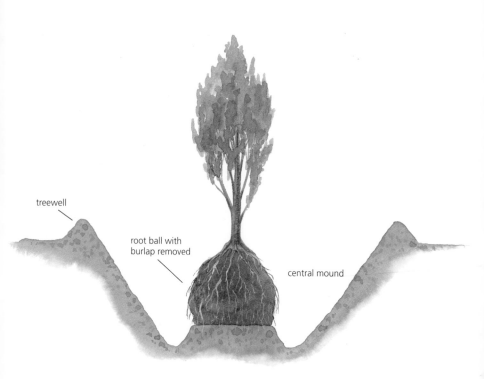

treewell

root ball with
burlap removed

central mound

Planting B&B stock

1. Gently remove container.

2. Ensure proper planting depth.

3. Backfill with amended soil.

4. Settle backfilled soil with water.

5. Ensure newly planted shrub is well watered.

6. Add mulch.

STAKING AND SUPPORTS

Some fruiting plants, for example, kiwi, require permanent support such as a trellis. A trellis is a lattice-work structure of criss-crossing strips of wood (or occasionally metal or heavy wire). It can be plain and inconspicuous or lavishly ornate. Grape vines can be trained to grow up a simple arbour, constructed with wood and wire or latticework. If the arbour is large enough, you might use it as a shady retreat as well. The sunny side of an open carport or porch can also provide support for grapes. Other supports include poles and pergolas. Any support should be erected before planting to avoid disturbing the roots of your new transplants.

Stakes provide support for your new tree transplants and should be inserted immediately after planting. An unstaked fruit or nut tree develops more roots and a stronger trunk. However, in windy locations, a tree taller than 1.5 m (5') will need some support until the roots are established to prevent it from being blown over.

Two common methods for staking newly planted trees are the two-stake method and the three-stake method. You can use wood or metal stakes for either method.

Use the two-stake method for small trees, 1.5–1.8 m (5–6') tall, and for trees in low-wind areas. Drive

stake in undisturbed soil

treewell

Two-stake method

stakes into the undisturbed soil just outside the planting hole on opposite sides of the tree. Staking any closer to the tree can damage roots and will not provide adequate support. Tie string, rope, cable or wire to the stakes and attach it to the tree about 90 cm–1.2 m (3–4') above the ground.

Larger trees and trees in areas with strong or shifting winds require the three-stake method. The technique is the same, but with three stakes evenly spaced around the tree.

For either method, never wrap a wire or cable directly around the tree trunk. Thread it through a piece of old garden hose or some other buffer to protect the trunk from damage. Allow some slack. Young trees need to move in the wind to strengthen their trunks and

develop thicker roots in appropriate areas to compensate for the prevailing wind. One year of staking is sufficient for almost all trees, and staking should be removed at that time.

Raspberries and other bramble fruits do well if trained to grow between wires. Drive in a sturdy stake or pole at each end of the row. Affix a horizontal crossbar (a piece of scrap wood works well) to each stake. Attach two wires to the crossbars and extend them on either side of the plants. These support wires will corral the canes and ensure a tidy, manageable row. The plants take up less room and the berries will be much easier to pick.

As mentioned earlier, wires or trellises are used to support espaliered trees. Here, too, the tree takes up much less room and is easier to harvest.

treewell

Three-stake method

CARING FOR FRUITING PLANTS

WATERING

Once established, many plants are drought tolerant, but new transplants need to be watered regularly; keep them moist during the first season, and don't let them dry out. A weekly deep watering, soaking down at least 10 cm (4"), is better than several shallow sprinkles. Deep, slow, infrequent watering encourages a stronger root system and adapts the plants to seeking out water trapped deep in the soil. The best time to water is in the early morning to reduce evaporation loss.

MULCHING

Mulch helps retain moisture and aids in keeping soil at a consistent temperature. Organic mulches include compost, bark chips, grass clippings and shredded leaves and will provide nutrients as they break down. Spread mulch 5–10 cm (2–4") thick, keeping it a slight distance away from the plants. Any material pressing against plants can trap moisture, prevent air circulation and encourage fungal disease. Replenish the mulch as it breaks down over summer.

Keep mulch away from the base of your plants

FEEDING

Organic mulch and compost get fruiting plants off to a good start, but adding fertilizer ensures bountiful crops at harvest time. Nutrients occur naturally in the soil, but depending on the health of your soil, it may still be lacking some essential nutrients for plant growth. Heavy feeders will definitely need additional supplements. Fertilizer comes in various forms, including liquids, water-soluble powders, slow-release granules or pellets and bulk materials such as compost.

Organic fertilizers can be simple or complex formulations. They may include alfalfa pellets, composted animal manure, crab meal, coconut meal, corn gluten, kelp meal, sunflower meal, rock phosphate, humus, leaf mould, bone meal, blood meal, earthworm castings, bird or bat guano, dolomite lime, pulverized oyster shells, glacial rock dust, greensand and beneficial mycorrhizal fungi. Note that bone meal, fish emulsion and other odorous organic fertilizers may attract unwanted garden visitors that can cause major destruction.

Organic fertilizers enhance the microorganism population in the planting mix, which in turn makes more nutrients available to the plants. Organic fertilizers don't work as quickly as many inorganic fertilizers, but they often don't leach out as quickly. They can be watered into planting mix or used as a foliar spray as often as weekly.

Fertilize very early in spring, prior to any real growth occurring. Follow the package directions carefully. Excessive fertilizer can burn roots and kill plants or stimulate excessive plant growth that is susceptible to pest and disease problems. Some plants may need multiple applications, but always reduce fertilizer applications in late summer or early autumn, depending on the region, to allow perennials, shrubs and trees time to harden off before the cold weather.

WEEDING

Weeds compete for light, nutrients and space. They can also harbour pests and diseases. Weed often. Weeding is much easier and less time consuming when the weeds are small. Also, if you get them when they're small, they won't have time to produce seeds that will cause trouble the following season.

Weeding is an important task

Overwintering

If your melons and other annual fruits haven't quite matured by the time the forecast includes frost, protecting plants to extend the growing season is relatively simple. Cover them overnight with sheets, towels, burlap, row covers or even cardboard boxes. Do not use plastic because it does not retain heat and therefore will not provide any insulation.

Tender plants, including tropicals, may have to be moved indoors in winter. Before the first frosts in autumn, bring your tender plants into the shelter of a greenhouse or the sunniest, warmest location in your house. Most tender plants can be treated as houseplants, whether they return outdoors the following season or not. If you don't have space to overwinter large tender plants indoors, take cuttings in late summer and grow them as smaller plants for the following spring.

Some gardeners will grow their tender plants in partial shade outdoors so that the plants will be accustomed to the lower light levels when brought inside for the winter.

Winter storage (above & below)

PRUNING

*P*runing can maintain the health of a plant, increase the quality and yield of fruit, control and direct growth, and create interesting plant forms and shapes such as espalier.

TOOLS

Using the right tools makes pruning easier and more effective. **Secateurs**, or hand pruners, should be used for snipping off excess runners, small suckers and cutting branches up to 2 cm (³/₄") in diameter. **Loppers** are long-handled pruners used for branches up to 4 cm (1¹/₂") in diameter. Loppers are also good for removing excess, damaged or weak canes from raspberries and other cane stock.

To make the cleanest cut, orient the secateurs or loppers so the blades are to the plant side of the cut and the hook is to the side of the branch or cane being removed. If the cut is made with the hook toward the plants, the cut will be ragged and slow to heal.

Pruning saws have teeth especially designed to cut through green wood. They can be used to cut branches up to 15 cm (6") in diameter and sometimes larger. Pruning saws are easier to use and much safer than chainsaws.

Make sure your tools are sharp and clean before you begin any pruning task. If the branch you are cutting is diseased, you will need to sterilize the tool before using it again. A solution of 1 part bleach to 10 parts water is effective for cleaning and sterilizing.

Pinching is simply pinching off soft, new growth to encourage more foliage or better blooms. The only tool you need for pinching is your thumb and forefinger.

Disbudding, carried out in spring, is the process of removing side buds before they are fully developed. Your thumb and forefinger, or a small knife, are also all that's required for disbudding. For plants such as roses, disbudding results in fewer but showier flowers.

Proper secateur orientation

PRUNING TIPS

In general, pruning raspberries and other bramble bushes is straightforward. In autumn, remove all the canes that have borne fruit. Make clean cuts close to the ground. Also cut out any damaged, weak or spindly canes, leaving only the thickest and healthiest canes. Top the remaining canes to a height that's convenient for picking. In spring, after the buds have swollen, cut the canes back to this height. Some growers recommend pinching the new shoots of black and purple raspberries to encourage lateral branches to grow from the main stem.

Roses should be pruned in late spring when the leaf buds have begun to swell and the danger of freezing weather has passed. Make a

Kiwi

slanting cut just above a bud that points to the outside rather than the inside of the plant to encourage open, healthier growth. Also remove diseased, damaged or spindly canes.

Blueberries produce fruit on the previous season's growth, and the most vigorous wood produces the biggest berries. Without pruning, berries will be undersized and there will be little new growth for the next year's crop. Begin pruning in the third season, spacing out equal numbers of one-, two- and three-year branches. Remove spreading branches growing at ground level. Keep the upright branches and, if the centre of the plant is becoming crowded, cut out any weak or older branches.

For red currants and gooseberries, start pruning in the fifth year, removing any canes older than four years. Also cut out old, low-growing branches and any that are diseased, weak or broken.

Grapes should be pruned annually, in late winter. As a rough guide, you want to leave an optimum number of canes growing from the main trunk and the permanent branches or "arms" to produce fruit later in the year. These canes will also provide buds to grow into new, well-positioned shoots that will provide fruit the following year.

For vines such as figs and kiwis, an annual pruning of overlong and excess branches will maintain a practical size and shape.

Pruning Fruit and Nut Trees

Care of fruit and nut trees is a bit more involved. Pruning them is possibly the most important maintenance task—and the easiest to mess up. If you're a new gardener with mature, but neglected trees, it may be best to initially call in an expert, such as a certified member of the International Society of Arborists (ISA). They have the knowledge and the specialty pruning equipment to do a proper job on a large, untended tree.

Once the tree is in good shape it's much easier for the home gardener to maintain. Pruning courses can give you the confidence to continue on your own and are offered by many garden centres, botanical societies and adult education programs.

If the tree is growing near a power line or other hazardous area, *always* call in a professional.

Fortunately, if you're starting out with young trees, good pruning techniques are not difficult to learn. In fact, if done correctly and continued on a regular basis, pruning can be quite enjoyable.

Aside from removing damaged branches, do not prune a fruit or nut tree for the first year after planting. After that time, the first pruning should begin to develop the structure of the tree. The goal is to maintain an open form so sunlight reaches the fruit. In the early years of the tree's life, you want to create a pleasing shape and a strong framework to bear and support the fruit. At this time you can also begin training the tree to a particular size or form, such as espalier.

For a strong framework, leave branches with a wide angle at the crotch (where the branch meets the trunk or another branch) because these branches are the strongest. Prune out branches with narrower crotches, while ensuring an even distribution of the main (scaffold) branches. These branches will support all future top growth.

English walnut

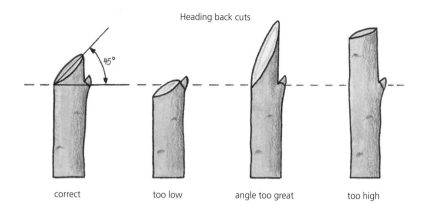

Heading back cuts

45°

correct   too low   angle too great   too high

THE KINDEST CUT

Trees have a remarkable ability to heal themselves. Proper pruning cuts allow the tree to heal as quickly as possible, preventing disease and insect attacks. A basic familiarity with the following cuts will help insure successful pruning.

Cutting back to a bud is used to shorten a branch, redirect growth or maintain the size of the tree. The cut should be made slightly less than 0.5 cm (1/4") above a bud. If the cut is too far away from or too close to the bud, the wound will not heal properly. Make sure to cut back to buds that are pointing in the direction in which you want the new growth to grow.

Cutting to a lateral branch is used to shorten limbs and redirect growth. This cut is similar to cutting back to a bud. The diameter of the branch to which you are cutting back must be at least one-third of the diameter of the branch you are cutting. The cut should be made slightly less than 0.5 cm (1/4") above the lateral branch and should line up with the angle of the branch. Make cuts at an angle whenever possible to prevent rain from seeping into the open wound.

Ensure the bud beneath each cut is pointing in the direction you want the branch to grow.

Heading back cuts

Cutting to a lateral branch

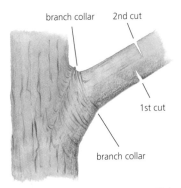

branch collar   2nd cut

1st cut

branch collar

3rd cut at
branch collar

Limb removal steps

Removing limbs can be a complicated operation. Because of the large size of the wound, it is critical to cut in the correct place—at the branch collar—to ensure quick healing. The cut must be done in steps to avoid damaging the bark. The first cut is on the bottom of the branch to be removed, a short distance from the trunk of the tree. The purpose of this cut is to prevent bark from peeling down the tree when the second cut causes the main part of the branch to fall. The first cut should be 30–45 cm (12–18") up from the branch collar and should extend one-third of the way through the branch. The second cut is made a bit farther along the branch from the first cut and is made from the top of the branch. This cut removes the majority of the branch. The final cut should be made just above the branch collar. The plant tissues at the branch collar quickly create a barrier to disease and insects. Some sources suggest using a sharp knife to bevel the edges of the cut to promote quicker healing.

The use of pruning paint or paste has been much debated. These substances may do more harm than good. Trees have a natural ability to compartmentalize dead and decaying sections, and an unpainted cut will eventually heal over. A cut that has been treated with paint or paste may never heal properly.

Heading back cuts

THINNING

Much like pruning, thinning is the removal of excess growth. Whereas pruning may remove only a section of a branch or cane, thinning is often defined as the complete removal of branches, stems or suckers, resulting in no new growth where the cut was made. Thinning can also refer to the removal of excess fruit.

Fruit trees initially set more fruit than they can ripen. This protects them from a late frost that might damage or kill some of the developing fruit. Once all danger of frost is past, the trees naturally shed excess fruit. Gardeners may choose to remove even more of the developing fruits to produce a larger and tastier crop. This type of thinning can reduce a heavy crop that threatens to break the bearing limb and also prevents "alternate bearing," the tendency of some fruit trees to alternate years of bearing very large, followed by very small, crops.

To thin apples, peaches and other tree fruits, remove excess developing fruits, or "fruitlets," as soon as they set, right after the tree blooms. Home gardeners may choose to do this in two steps. Remove some of the fruit and then, as insurance, wait until the tree completes its own fruit drop before removing any additional fruitlets. Whether you thin all at once or in two steps, thin selectively. Remove the smallest fruitlets and any that are diseased or damaged by insects. Small fruits such as cherries do not need to be thinned.

Thinning cuts

PROPAGATION

*P*ropagating your own plants is an interesting and challenging aspect of gardening that can save you money, but it also takes time, space and effort. Besides dividing, other ways of increasing plants is with seeds or cuttings or by layering.

SEEDS

Starting from seed is a great way to propagate a large number of plants at a relatively low cost. Seeds can be purchased or collected from your own or a friend's garden. However, propagating from seed has its limitations. Some cultivars and varieties don't pass on their desirable traits to their offspring. Apple is a good example of a fruit that does not grow true from seed. Others take a very long time to germinate, if they germinate at all, and an even longer time to grow to a fruiting size.

DIVIDING

Division is perhaps the easiest way to propagate perennials. Dividing your plants not only keeps their size under control and rejuvenates the plant, it is also a means of propagation. Each division becomes its own plant.

As most perennials grow, they form larger and larger clumps. Dividing this clump periodically will rejuvenate the plant, keep its size in check and provide you with more plants.

In general, watch for these signs that indicate a perennial may need dividing:
• The centre of the plant has died out
• The plant is no longer flowering or fruiting as profusely as it did in previous years
• The plant is encroaching on the growing space of other plants sharing the bed.

Pulling a clump apart

Cutting apart and dividing tuberous plants (above & below)

It is relatively easy to divide perennials. Begin by digging up the entire clump and knocking any large clods of soil away from the root ball. The clump can then be split into several pieces. A small plant with fibrous roots can be torn into sections by hand. A large plant can be pried apart with a pair of garden forks inserted back to back into the clump. Plants with thicker tuberous or rhizomatous roots can be cut into sections with a sharp, sterile knife. In all cases, cut away any old sections that have died out and replant only the newer, more vigorous sections.

Once your clump has been divided into sections, replant one or two of them into the original location. The other sections can be moved to new spots in the garden or potted and given to gardening friends and neighbours. Get the sections back into the ground as quickly as possible to prevent the exposed roots from drying out. Water new transplants thoroughly and keep them well watered until they have reestablished themselves.

Prickly pear, which can be started from seed, can also be propagated by a type of "division." Simply detach a pad from the mother plant and leave it to dry in a warm, sunny place. In a few days, the base should be completely dry and forming a callus. Pot up the pad in sandy compost, where it will quickly begin to root.

Removing lower leaves

Cuttings

Cuttings are an excellent way to propagate varieties and cultivars that you really like but that don't come true from seed or that don't produce seed at all. Each cutting will grow into a reproduction of the parent plant. Cuttings are taken from the stems of some plants and the roots of others.

STEM CUTTINGS

Stem cuttings are generally taken in spring and early summer and are sometimes referred to as softwood stem cuttings. During this time, plants go through a flush of fresh, new growth, either before or after flowering. Avoid taking cuttings from plants that are in flower. Plants that are in flower, or that are about to flower, are busy trying to reproduce; plants that are busy growing, by contrast, are already full of the right hormones to promote quick root growth. If you do take cuttings from plants that are flowering, be sure to remove the flowers and the buds to divert the plant's energy back into growing. Fruits that reproduce well from stem cuttings include Oregon grapeholly, juniper, ginkgo, passionflower and kiwi. Fruit trees such as peach, nectarine and plum can also be propagated from softwood cuttings. Gooseberries, serviceberries and blueberries are also easily started this way.

Cuttings need to be kept in a warm, humid place to root, which makes them very prone to fungal diseases. Providing proper sanitation and encouraging quick rooting will increase the survival rate of your cuttings.

Debate exists over what the size of a cutting should be. Some gardeners claim that a smaller cutting of 2–5 cm (1–2") long is more likely to root and to root more quickly. Others claim that a larger cutting of 10–15 cm (4–6") develops more roots and becomes established more quickly once planted in the garden. Try different sizes and use whatever works for you.

The size of a cutting is determined by the number of leaf nodes that it has. There should be at least three or four nodes on a cutting. The node is where the leaf joins the stem, and it is from there that the new roots will grow. The base of the cutting should be just below a node. Strip the leaves gently from the first and second nodes, and plant the cutting so those nodes are below the soil. The new

Dipping in rooting hormone

Firming the cutting into the soil

plants will grow from the nodes above the soil. The leaves can be left in place on the cutting above ground. If there is a lot of space between nodes, your cutting will be longer than recommended. Some plants have almost no space at all between nodes. Cut these plants to the recommended length, and gently remove the leaves from the lower half of the cutting. Plants with several nodes close together often root quickly and abundantly.

Always use a sharp, sterile knife to make the cuttings. Cuts should be made straight across the stem. Once you have stripped the leaves, you can dip the end of the cutting into a rooting hormone powder intended for softwood cuttings. Sprinkle the powder onto a piece of paper and dip the cuttings into it. Discard any extra powder left on the paper to prevent the spread of disease. Tap or blow the extra powder off the cutting. Cuttings caked with rooting hormone are more likely to rot rather than root, and they do not root any faster than those that are lightly dusted. Your cuttings are now prepared for planting.

The sooner you plant your cuttings, the better. The less water the cuttings lose, the less likely they are to wilt and the more quickly they will root. Cuttings can be planted in a similar manner to seeds. Use sterile soil mix intended for seeds or cuttings in pots or trays that can be covered with plastic to keep in the humidity. Other mixes you can use to root cuttings are sterilized sand, perlite, vermiculite or a combination of the three. Press the soil mix down and moisten it before you start planting. Poke a hole in the surface of the soil mix with a pencil or similar object, tuck the cutting in and gently press the soil mix around it. Make sure the

Newly planted cuttings

lowest leaves do not touch the soil mix and that the cuttings are spaced far enough apart that adjoining leaves do not touch each other. Pots can be placed inside plastic bags. Push stakes or wires into the soil around the edge of the pot so that the plastic will be held off the leaves. The rigid plastic lids that are available for trays may not be high enough to fit over the cuttings, in which case you will have to use stakes and a plastic bag to cover the tray.

Keep the cuttings in a warm place, about 18–21° C (65–70° F), in bright, indirect light. A couple of holes poked in the bag will allow for some ventilation. Turn the bag inside out when condensation becomes heavy. Keep the soil mix moist. A hand-held mister will gently moisten the soil mix without disturbing the cuttings.

Most cuttings will require one to four weeks to root. After two weeks, gently tug the cutting. You will feel resistance if roots have formed. If the cutting feels as though it can be pulled out of the soil mix, gently push it back down and leave it for longer. New growth is also a good sign that your cutting has rooted. Some gardeners simply leave the cuttings alone until they can see roots through the holes in the bottoms of the pots. Uncover the cuttings once they have developed roots.

Apply a foliar feed with a hand-held mister when the cuttings are showing new leaf growth. Plants quickly absorb nutrients through the leaves; therefore, you can avoid stressing the newly formed roots. Your local garden centre should have foliar feeds and information about applying them.

Once your cuttings are rooted and have had a chance to become established, they can be potted up individually. If you rooted several cuttings in one pot or tray, you may find that the roots have tangled together. If gentle pulling doesn't separate them, take the entire tangled clump and try rinsing some of the soil away. You should be able to free the roots enough to separate the plants.

Pot the young plants in a sterile potting soil. They can be moved into a sheltered area of the garden or a cold frame and grown in pots until they are large enough to plant in the garden. The plants may need some protection over the first winter. Keep them in the cold frame if they are still in pots. Give them an extra layer of mulch if they have been planted out.

Healthy roots

HARDWOOD CUTTINGS

Grapes and many fruit trees and berry plants are propagated with hardwood cuttings. These cuttings are taken in late autumn when the plants are dormant. Select disease-free stock that has never been damaged by frost or insects. Take pencil-thickness cuttings by making a clean, diagonal cut above a tip bud and a lower bud. Cuttings should be about 13–23 cm (5–9") long with some older wood at the base.

Secure cuttings in bundles of a dozen twigs, with the bottom ends even, and bury them outdoors in light, sandy soil. Place them below the frost line, about 60 cm (24") deep. In spring, you'll hopefully discover a callus has formed on the bottom of the cuttings. Plant each cutting individually and deeply in a lightly shaded, temporary spot. Once the cuttings have rooted and are producing leaves, they can be moved and planted in a permanent location.

BASAL CUTTINGS

Basal cuttings involve removing the new growth from the main clump and rooting it in the same manner as stem cuttings. Many plants, such as raspberries and currants, send up new shoots or plantlets around their bases. Often, the plantlets will already have a few roots growing. The young plants develop quickly and may even grow to flowering size the first summer. You may have to cut back some of the top growth of the shoot because the tiny developing roots won't be able to support a lot of top growth. Treat these cuttings in the same way you would a stem cutting. Use a sterile knife to cut out the shoot. Sterile soil mix and humid conditions are preferred. Pot plants individually or place them in soft soil in the garden until new growth appears and roots have developed.

Raspberries

ROOT CUTTINGS

Root cuttings can be taken from plants such as blackberry, raspberry, elderberry, currant, gooseberry and sumac. The main difference between starting root cuttings and stem cuttings is that root cuttings must be kept fairly dry because they can rot very easily.

Cuttings should be taken in early or mid-spring when the ground is just starting to warm up and the roots are just about to break dormancy. At this time, the roots are full of nutrients, which the plants stored the previous summer and autumn, and hormones are initiating growth. You may have to moisten the soil around the plant so that you can loosen it enough to get to the roots.

Keep the roots slightly moist, but not wet, while you are rooting them, and keep track of which end is up. Roots must be planted in a vertical, not horizontal, position in the soil, and they need to be kept in the orientation they held when attached to the parent plant. Gardeners use different tricks to differentiate the top from the bottom of the roots. One method is to cut straight across the tops and diagonally across the bottoms.

You do not want very young or very old roots. Very young roots are usually white and quite soft; very old roots are tough and woody. The roots you should use will be tan-coloured and still fleshy. To prepare your root, cut out the section you will be using with a sterile knife. Cut the root into pieces that are 2.5–5 cm (1–2") long.

Remove any side roots before planting the sections in pots or planting trays. You can use the same type of soil mix that seeds and stem cuttings were started in. Poke the pieces vertically into the soil, and leave a tiny bit of the end sticking up out of the soil. Remember to keep the pieces the right way up.

Keep the pots or trays in a warm place out of direct sunlight. Avoid overwatering them. They will send up new shoots once they have rooted, and they can be planted in the same manner as the stem cuttings.

Sumac

Layering

Layering is the easiest method of propagating new plants and the one most likely to produce successful results. Layering allows future cuttings to form their own roots before they are removed from the parent plant. Various methods of layering, including mound, trench and tip layering, lend themselves to increasing your stock of fruit plants.

MOUND LAYERING

Mound layering is a simple way to propagate low, shrubby plants. With this technique, the shrub is partially buried in a mound of well-drained soil mix. The buried stems will then sprout roots along their lengths. Quince can be reproduced this way.

Mound layering should be initiated in spring, once new shoots begin to grow. Make a mound from a mixture of sand, peat moss and soil over half or more of the plant. Leave the tips of the branches exposed. More soil can be mounded up over the course of summer. Keep the mound moist, but not soggy. At the end of summer, gently wash the mound away and detach the rooted branches. Plant into a permanent spot or in a protected, temporary location if you want to shelter them for the first winter.

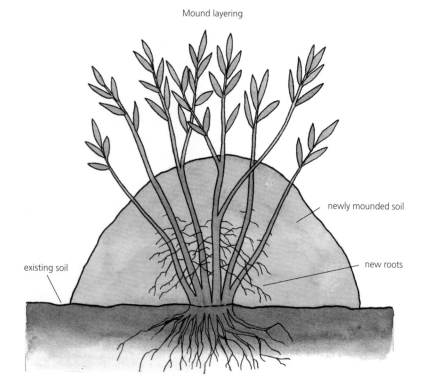

Mound layering

existing soil

newly mounded soil

new roots

TIP LAYERING

Tip layering works with plants with long flexible branches such as raspberry, currant and gooseberry. In early summer, bend branches to the ground, make a small cut in each branch and bury the cut area under 5–8 cm (2–3") of soil. Allow the branch tips to protrude. By autumn, the branches should have formed roots and can be cut from the main plant and replanted in their new spots.

TRENCH LAYERING

Trench layering works with plants such as grape and blackberry that have long, flexible branches. In July, select a slender branch, remove all the leaves except a few at the tip, and lightly nick the branch in two or three places. Lay the branch in a shallow, 15 cm (6") deep trench, anchor with a hairpin-shaped wire and cover with 8–10 cm (3–4") of soil. Again, let the branch tip protrude. Roots should form where the bark was nicked, and once this occurs, cut the branch into individual plants and settle them into their new garden homes.

Trench layering

pebble to keep slit open

rock for extra weight

wire to hold branch

GRAFTING

Grafting is the surgical union of two different but related living plants. This technique is often used to propagate fruit trees and can also be used to repair damaged trees. For the small home garden, grafting allows several varieties of a particular tree fruit, such as pears, apples or plums, to be grown on the same tree. Grafting also gives the option of choosing the rootstock, which governs the mature size of the tree, be it dwarf, semi-dwarf or standard size.

Stories of apple trees bearing plums and cherries or, even more fantastically, tomatoes, are just tall tales. For successful grafts, the scion (or transferred part) must be taken from a close botanical cousin to the stock (or rooted section). Stone fruit such as apricot will unite with other stone fruit such as peach or plum. It will not take with a pome fruit such as apple.

Much of the fruit tree stock you purchase from a nursery will have been grafted. There are many methods of grafting, each more appropriate to a particular type of tree or a geographical area than another. As well, some methods are easier for the home gardener's first attempt. Since it's often years before your fruit tree will bear and you realize the success of your graft, it's best to acquire as much instruction beforehand as possible. Get advice from an experienced grafter in your area or, better yet, sign up for a hands-on grafting class. Adult education programs and nursery centres often offer workshops.

Plums

PESTS AND DISEASES

Gardens often contain a mixture of different plant species. Because many insects and diseases attack only one species of plant, mixed gardens make it difficult for pests and diseases to find their preferred hosts and establish a population. At the same time, because the plants are in the same spot for many years, the problems can become permanent. Luckily, beneficial insects, birds and other pest-devouring organisms can also develop permanent populations to help keep pests and diseases under control.

For many years, pest control meant spraying or dusting. The goal was to try to eliminate every pest in the garden. A more moderate approach is advocated today. The goal now is to maintain problems at levels at which only negligible damage is done. Synthetic pesticides should be used only

as a last resort because they can cause more harm than good. They endanger gardeners and their families and pets, and they kill the good organisms as well as the bad ones, leaving the garden open to even worse attacks.

Managing pests organically involves four steps. Cultural controls are the most important, followed by physical controls, then biological controls. Chemical controls should be used only when the first three have been exhausted. If you're compelled to use a pesticide, it is imperative that you follow the directions and cover yourself with appropriate protective gear.

Cultural controls are the regular techniques you use in the day-to-day care of your garden. Growing plants in the conditions they prefer and keeping your soil healthy with plenty of organic matter are two cultural

Frogs eat many insect pests

Predatory ground beetle

controls you can use to keep pests manageable in your garden. Choose resistant varieties of plants that are not prone to problems. Space them so that there is good air circulation around them and the plants are not stressed from competition for light, nutrients and room to grow. Remove plants from the garden if they are constantly decimated by the same pests every year. Remove and destroy diseased foliage, and prevent the spread of disease by keeping your gardening tools clean and by tidying up fallen leaves and dead plant matter at the end of the growing season.

Physical controls are generally used to combat insect problems. They include picking insects off by hand, which is not as daunting as it seems if you catch the problem when it is just beginning. Other physical controls are barriers that stop the pests from getting to the plant or traps that either catch or confuse the pest. The physical control of diseases can generally only be accomplished by removing the infected plant parts to prevent the spread of the problem.

Biological controls make use of natural predators, including birds, snakes, frogs, spiders, lady beetles and certain bacteria. Encourage

Ladybird beetle

these creatures to take up permanent residence in your garden. A birdbath and birdfeeder will encourage birds to enjoy your yard and feed on a wide variety of insect pests. Many beneficial insects probably already live in your garden, and they can be encouraged to stay with alternate food sources. Although beneficial insects may enjoy feeding on the fruits you're trying to grow, many also eat the nectar from flowers. The flowers of nectar plants such as yarrow, sea holly and purple coneflower are popular with some predatory insects, and you might choose to grow them for the health of your fruit-bearing plants.

Chemical controls should be used as a last resort, but if it does become necessary to use them, some organic options are available. Organic sprays are no less dangerous than inorganic ones, but they will break down into harmless compounds because they come from natural sources. The main drawback to using any chemicals is that they may also kill the beneficial insects you have been trying to attract to your garden. Organic chemicals are available at local garden centres and should be applied at the rates and for the pests recommended on the packages. Proper and early identification of problems is vital for finding a quick solution.

Whereas cultural, physical, biological and chemical controls are all possible defences against insects, diseases must be controlled culturally. Prevention is often the only hope. A healthy, unaffected plant is much less vulnerable than one that is diseased, infested with pests or that has a number of other problems. Once a plant has been infected, it should probably be destroyed to prevent the spread of the disease.

Butterfly

Green aphids (above, Japanese beetles (below)

PESTS

APHIDS
Cluster along stems, on buds and on leaves. Tiny, pear-shaped, winged or wingless; green, black, brown, red or grey. Suck sap from plants, causing distorted or stunted growth; sticky honeydew forms on the surfaces and encourages sooty mould.

What to Do: Squish small colonies by hand; dislodge with brisk water spray; spray serious infestations with insecticidal soap; many predatory insects and birds feed on them.

BEETLES AND WEEVILS
Some, such as lady beetles, are beneficial; others, such as June beetles, eat plants. Many types and sizes; usually round with hard, shell-like outer wings covering membranous inner wings. Leave wide range of chewing damage; cause small or large holes in or around margins of leaves; entire leaf or areas between leaf veins is consumed; may also chew holes in flowers. Larvae: see Borers

What to Do: Pick them off at night and drop them into an old coffee can half filled with soapy water (soap prevents them from floating); spread an old sheet under plants and shake off beetles to collect and dispose of them.

BIRDS
Often attracted to ripening fruit, which they damage by eating.

What to Do: Cover ripening fruit crops, such as cherries, with netting until harvest. Deter birds with loud noises, plastic predator birds such as owls, or bright, dangling objects such as disposable aluminum pie pans or reflective tape or ribbon.

BORERS

Larvae of some moths and beetles. Worm-like; vary in size and get bigger as they bore through plants. Burrow into plant stems, leaves and/or roots. May see tunnels in leaves, stems or roots; stems weaken and may break; leaves wilt; rhizomes may be hollowed out entirely or in part.

What to Do: Remove and destroy affected parts; try squishing borers within leaves; may need to dig up and destroy infected roots and rhizomes.

BUGS

Many are beneficial; a few are pests. Small, up to 1 cm (1/2") long; green, brown, black or brightly coloured and patterned. Pierce plants to suck out sap; toxins may be injected that deform plants; sunken areas are left where pierced; leaves rip as they grow; leaves, buds and new growth may be dwarfed and deformed.

What to Do: Remove debris and weeds from around plants in autumn to destroy overwintering sites; pick off by hand and drop into soapy water; spray with insecticidal soap.

Foliage chewed by beetles (above)
Skeletonizer damage (below)

CATERPILLARS

Larvae of some moths, butterflies and sawflies; include bagworms, leaf rollers and cutworms. Chew foliage and buds; can completely defoliate a plant if infestation is severe. Tent caterpillars and smaller webworms lay eggs in white masses on undersides of leaves. Spin white, silky webs or nests at ends of branches. Will severely damage or kill fruit and nut trees.

What to Do: Pick off by hand or, in the case of tent caterpillars, cut off nests, burn them and clean up debris around trees. Control biologically using the naturally occurring soil bacterium *Bacillus thuringiensis* var. *kurstaki* or *B.t.k.* (commercially available), which breaks down the gut lining of caterpillars. Remove nearby wild cherry and apple trees.

CODDLING MOTHS

Larvae white, about 2.5 cm (1") long. Adult moths grey-brown with fringed hind wings. Serious apple pests. Also infest various other fruit and nut trees.

What to Do: Dislodge larvae with a strong stream of water. Soapy water and fish oil sprays may also work. Attract woodpeckers to eat them.

Mealybugs (above), caterpillar (below)

CUTWORMS

Larvae of some moths. About 2.5 cm (1") long, plump, smooth-skinned caterpillars; curl up when poked or disturbed. Usually only affect young plants and seedlings, which may be completely consumed or chewed off at ground level.

What to Do: Create barriers from old toilet tissue rolls to make collars around plant bases; push tubes at least halfway into ground.

DEER

Can decimate crops; kill saplings by rubbing antlers on them; girdle tree bark or snap trees in two. Hosts for ticks that carry Lyme disease and Rocky Mountain spotted fever.

What to Do: Many deterrents work for a while. Encircle immature shrubs or trees with tall, upright sticks; place dangling soap bars around the garden; use noise-making devices or water spritzers to startle deer; mount flashy aluminum or moving devices throughout the garden.

LEAFHOPPERS

Small, wedge-shaped insects; green, brown, grey or multi-coloured; jump around frantically when disturbed. Suck juice from plant leaves; cause distorted growth; carry diseases such as aster yellows.

What to Do: Encourage predators by planting nectar-producing species such as yarrow, sea holly and purple coneflower. Wash off insects with a strong spray of water; spray with insecticidal soap or neem oil according to package directions.

LEAFMINERS

Larvae of some flies; tiny, yellow or green, stubby maggots. Tunnel within leaves, leaving winding trails; tunnelled areas are a lighter colour than rest of leaf. Unsightly rather than a health risk to plants.

What to Do: Remove and destroy infected foliage; remove debris from area in autumn to destroy overwintering sites; attract parasitic wasps with nectar plants such as sea holly.

LEAF SKELETONIZERS
see Beetles and Weevils

NEMATODES

Tiny, worm-like organisms; one type infects foliage and stems, other type infects roots. *Foliar:* yellow spots on leaves that turn brown; leaves shrivel and wither; problem starts on lowest leaves and works up. *Root knot:* plant is stunted and may wilt; yellow spots on leaves; roots have tiny bumps or knots.

What to Do: Remove infected plants. Mulch soil and clean up debris in autumn; don't touch wet foliage; add organic matter and parasitic nematodes to soil. Not a problem throughout areas where the ground freezes too deeply for pests to overwinter.

Leafminer damage

Large slug

SCALE INSECTS

Soft-bodied, tiny, crawling insects that include mealybugs; related to aphids; appear to be covered with white fuzz or flour. Sucking damage stunts and stresses plant; excrete honeydew that promotes growth of sooty mould.

What to Do: Remove by hand from smaller plants; wash plant with soap and water or wipe with alcohol-soaked swabs; remove heavily infested leaves; encourage or introduce natural predators such as mealybug destroyer beetles and parasitic wasps; spray with insecticidal soap.

SLUGS AND SNAILS

Slugs lack shells; snails have a spiral shell; smooth, grey, green, black, beige, yellow or spotted. Leave large, ragged holes in leaves and silvery slime trails on and around plants.

What to Do: Attach strips of copper to wood around raised beds or smaller boards inserted around susceptible groups of plants; slugs and snails will get a shock if they try to cross copper surfaces. Pick them off by hand in the evening; spread wood ash or diatomaceous earth (available from garden centres) on ground around plants to pierce their soft bodies and cause them to dehydrate.

SPIDER MITES

Almost invisible to the naked eye; relatives of spiders without their insect-eating habits. Tiny, eight-legged; red, yellow or green; may spin webs. Usually found on under-sides of plant leaves. Suck juice out of leaves; may see fine webbing on leaves and stems; may see mites moving on leaf undersides; leaves become discoloured and speckled, then turn brown and shrivel up.

What to Do: Wash them off with a strong spray of water daily until all signs of infestation are gone; preda-tory mites are available through gar-den centres; spray plants with insecticidal soap.

WHITEFLIES

Flying insects that flutter up into the air when the plant is disturbed. Tiny, moth-like, white; live on undersides of plant leaves. Suck juice out of plant leaves, causing yellowed leaves and weakened plants; leave sticky honeydew on leaves, which encour-ages sooty mould.

What to Do: Destroy weeds where insects may live; attract native preda-tory beetles and parasitic wasps with nectar plants such as sea holly, yar-row and purple coneflower; spray severe cases with insecticidal soap.

DISEASES

ANTHRACNOSE

Fungus. Yellow or brown spots on leaves; sunken lesions and blisters on stems; can kill plant.

What to Do: Choose resistant variet-ies and cultivars; remove and destroy infected plant parts; thin out stems to improve air circulation; avoid handling wet foliage; keep soil well drained; clean up and destroy mate-rial from infected plants at end of growing season.

ASTER YELLOWS

Transmitted by leafhoppers. Stunted or deformed growth; leaves yellowed and deformed; flowers dwarfed and greenish; can kill plant.

What to Do: Control insects with insecticidal soap or neem oil spray according to package directions; remove and destroy infected plants; destroy any local weeds sharing symptoms.

BLACKSPOT

see Leaf Spot

BLIGHT

Fungal or bacterial diseases; many types, e.g., leaf blight, snow blight, tip blight. Leaves, stems and flowers blacken, rot and die.

What to Do: Thin stems to improve air circulation; keep mulch away from base of plants; remove debris from garden at end of growing sea-son. Remove and destroy infected plant parts.

CANKER

Caused by a virus or bacteria; can affect fruit and nut trees as well as some berries. Noticeable, diseased wound on wood; may spread around trunk and kill tree.

What to Do: Cut out diseased wood; sterilize tools with chlorine bleach solution.

GALLS

Unusual swellings of plant tissues that may be caused by insects or diseases. Can affect leaves, buds, stems, flowers or fruit; often a specific gall affects a single genus or species.

What to Do: Cut out galls from plant and destroy them; a gall caused by an insect usually contains the insect's eggs and juvenile stages. Prevent such galls by controlling insects before they lay eggs; otherwise try to remove and destroy the infected tissue before young insects emerge. Insect galls are generally more unsightly than damaging to plants; galls caused by disease often require destruction of plants. Don't place other plants susceptible to same disease in that location.

Tiny galls on upper leaf surface

GREY MOULD (BOTRYTIS BLIGHT)

Fungus. Leaves, stems and flowers blacken, rot and die.

What to Do: Remove and destroy infected plant parts; thin stems to improve air circulation; keep mulch away from base of plant, particularly in spring when plant starts to sprout; remove debris from garden at end of growing season.

LEAF SCORCH

Occurs when leaves lose water faster than it can be replaced. Signs include browning of leaf margins and yellowing or darkening of tissues between main leaf veins; leaves may dry up, turn brown and become brittle; sometimes rapid wilt, with leaves remaining pale green even when dried out. Damage often more pronounced on top, south-facing and windward portions of trees.

Powdery mildew

Caused by transplant shock, drought, herbicide injury, compacted soil and/or nutrient deficiency.

What to Do: Prune diseased areas; provide adequate water and nutrients; water deeply; site plants with consideration for their environment.

LEAF SPOT

Bacterial: small, brown or purple speckles grow to encompass entire leaves; leaves may drop. *Fungal:* black, brown or yellow spots cause leaves to wither.

What to Do: *Bacterial:* remove entire plant. *Fungal:* remove and destroy infected plant parts; sterilize removal tools; avoid wetting foliage or touching wet foliage; remove debris at end of growing season.

MILDEW

Two types, both fungal but with slightly different symptoms. *Downy mildew:* yellow spots on upper sides of leaves; yellow, white or grey downy fuzz on undersides. *Powdery mildew:* white or grey powdery coating on leaf surfaces that doesn't brush off.

What to Do: Choose resistant cultivars; space plants well; thin stems to encourage air circulation; remove and destroy infected leaves or other parts; tidy any debris in autumn.

MOSAIC

see Viruses

ROT

Several different fungi that affect different parts of plant. *Crown rot:* affects base of plant; stems blacken and fall over; leaves turn yellow and wilt; can kill plant. *Root rot:* leaves yellow; plant wilts; digging up plant will show roots rotted away.

What to Do: Keep soil well drained; don't damage plant if you are digging around it; keep mulches away from plant base; destroy infected plants.

RUST

Fungus. Pale spots on upper leaf surfaces; orange, fuzzy or dusty spots on leaf undersides.

What to Do: Destroy infected plant parts; choose rust-resistant varieties and cultivars; avoid handling wet leaves; provide plant with good air circulation; clear up garden debris at end of growing season.

SOOTY MOULD

Fungus. Thin, black film forms on leaf surfaces, reducing the amount of light reaching leaf surfaces.

What to Do: Wipe mould off leaf surfaces; control insects such as aphids and whiteflies that deposit honeydew on leaves, which forms mould.

VIRUSES

Plant may be stunted and leaves and flowers distorted, streaked or discoloured. Viral diseases in plants cannot be controlled.

What to Do: Destroy infected plants; control insects such as aphids, leafhoppers and whiteflies, which spread disease.

WILT

If watering hasn't helped, consider these two fungi. *Fusarium wilt:* plant wilts, leaves turn yellow then die; symptoms generally appear first on one part of plant before spreading to other parts. *Verticillium wilt:* plant wilts, leaves curl up at edges, turn yellow then drop off; plant may die.

What to Do: Both types of wilt are difficult to control. Choose resistant varieties and cultivars; clean up debris at end of growing season; destroy infected plants; solarize soil before replanting (may help if you've lost an entire bed of plants to these fungi).

Mosaic virus

Pest Control Alternatives

The following treatments for pests and diseases allow you some measure of control without resorting to harmful chemical fungicides and pesticides.

ANT CONTROL

Mix 750 mL (3 cups) water, 250 mL (1 cup) white sugar and 20 mL (4 tsp) liquid boric acid in a pot. Bring mixture just to a boil and remove it from heat. Let cool. Pour small amounts of the cooled mixture into bottlecaps or other very small containers and place them around the ant-infested area. You can also try setting out a mixture of equal parts powdered borax and icing sugar (no water).

ANTITRANSPIRANTS

These products were developed to reduce water transpiration, or loss of water, in plants. The waxy polymers surround fungal spores, preventing the spread of spores to nearby leaves and stems. When applied according to label directions, these products are environmentally friendly. They are available at garden centres.

BAKING SODA AND CITRUS OIL

This mixture treats both leaf spot and powdery mildew. In a spray bottle, mix 20 mL (4 tsp) baking soda and 15 mL (1 Tbsp) citrus oil in 4 L (1 gal) water. Spray foliage lightly, including undersides. Do not pour or spray directly onto soil.

Sticky pheromone traps are useful for monitoring insect populations

BAKING SODA AND HORTICUL-TURAL OIL

Research has confirmed the effectiveness of this mixture against powdery mildew. Mix 20 mL (4 tsp) baking soda and 15 mL (1 Tbsp) horticultural oil in 4 L (1 gal) water. Fill a spray bottle and spray foliage lightly, including undersides. Do not pour or spray directly onto soil.

COFFEE SPRAY

Boil 1 kg (2 lb) used coffee grounds in 13 L (3 gal) water for about 10 minutes. Allow to cool; strain the grounds out. Apply as a spray to reduce problems with whiteflies.

COMPOST TEA

Mix 500 g–1 kg (1–2 lb) compost in 22 L (5 gal) of water. Let sit for four to seven days. Dilute mix with water until it resembles weak tea. Use during normal watering, or apply as a foliar spray to prevent or treat fungal diseases.

FISH EMULSION, SEAWEED (KELP)

These products are usually used as foliar nutrient feeds but appear to also work against fungal diseases, either by preventing the fungus from spreading to noninfected areas or by changing the growing conditions for the fungus.

GARLIC SPRAY

This spray is an effective, organic means of controlling aphids, leafhoppers, whiteflies and some fungi and nematodes. Soak 90 mL (6 Tbsp) finely minced garlic in 10 mL (2 tsp) mineral oil for at least 24 hours. Add 500 mL (2 cups) water and 7 mL (1½ tsp) mild liquid dish soap. Stir and strain into a glass container for storage. Combine 15–30 mL (1–2 Tbsp) of this concentrate with 500 mL (2 cups) water to make a spray. Test spray on a few leaves, and check after two days for any damage. If no damage occurs, spray infested plants thoroughly, ensuring good coverage of foliage.

HORTICULTURAL OIL

Mix 75 mL (5 Tbsp) horticultural oil in 4 L (1 gal) water, and apply as a spray for a variety of insect and fungal problems.

INSECTICIDAL SOAP

Mix 5 mL (1 tsp) mild dish detergent or pure soap (biodegradable options are available) with 1 L (1 qt) water in a clean spray bottle. Spray the surfaces of insect-infested plants, and rinse well within an hour of spraying to avoid foliage discolouration.

NEEM OIL

Neem oil is derived from the neem tree (native to India) and is used as an insecticide, miticide and fungicide. It is most effective when used preventively. Apply when conditions are favourable for disease development. Neem is harmless to most beneficial insects and microorganisms.

SULPHUR AND LIME-SULPHUR

These products are good as preventive measures for fungal diseases. You can purchase ready-made products or wettable powders that you mix yourself. Do not spray when the temperature is expected to be 32° C (90° F) or higher, or you may damage your plants.

Larvae spinning a web at the tip of a conifer

The Conservatory

The delightfully named "orangerie" or conservatory has a long and varied history. The Hanging Gardens of Babylon could be considered one of the first notable structures for displaying and protecting plants. The exhibition of various botanicals also played a role in ancient Greece, Egypt and Asia.

Meaning "a place to store or preserve," the conservatory, as we think of it today, likely began in Roman times. Stone structures, fitted with mica, were an attempt to protect plants or crops but also let in light. During the Renaissance, timber sheds were constructed to protect tender plants, and later, in the 1600s, simple stone structures were again used. But the true glory days of the conservatory began in Victorian England.

At that time, travel and the procurement of exotic plants from warmer climes was a favourite pastime of the wealthy and the learned. The botanical treasures, once brought home, required a building of some type to protect them from Britain's cool weather. Soon, the glass-paned conservatory became a status symbol. Growing tropical fruit such as oranges was all the rage, leading to the name "orangerie."

The thin glass panes, taxed by weight, and the wrought iron to support them were costly. However, abolition of the glass tax in 1845 and the eventual development of steel, which was harder and better suited for roof supports, led to even greater interest in the conservatory.

The Great Conservatory, built at Chatsworth House, covered three-quarters of an acre. Its designer, Joseph Paxton, went on to create the renowned Crystal Palace in London, England. Built in less than a year for the Great Exhibition of 1851, the Crystal Palace required thousands of glass panes and covered 19 acres. For its time, the massive conservatory was the largest enclosed structure on earth.

Paxton was knighted for his efforts, and soon the middle class was clamouring for a modestly scaled, glazed addition to their homes. Sadly, the tremendous popularity of the conservatory was eventually its downfall. The once-grand structures became smaller and smaller and, as they became common and relatively affordable, they fell out of favour.

The Palm House at Kew Gardens is considered the most important surviving Victorian glass and iron structure. By the 1920s, most of the older, cast-iron conservatories had crumbled from frost and rust damage. It was not until the 1970s, with the advent of technological advances in glass and construction techniques, that the conservatory once again flourished. Today, the conservatory is more likely to be called a sunroom and used as additional living space, for relaxing or housing a spa, or as an exercise room. Still, the sunroom's abundance of natural light and a temperature-controlled environment is perfect for growing oranges—or other fruits.

ABOUT THIS GUIDE

*T*he plants in this book are organized alphabetically by their most familiar common name, which in some cases is the proper botanical name. If you are familiar with only the common name for a plant, you will still be able to find the plant easily in the book. The botanical name is always listed (in italics) under the common name(s). We strongly encourage you to learn and use these botanical names. A number of very different plants may share the same common name, and common names change from province to province. Only the botanical name for a plant defines exactly what plant it is, everywhere on the planet and in any language.

Clearly indicated at the beginning of each entry are height and spread ranges, as well as flower colour, bloom time and hardiness zones. Zone information indicates the overall hardiness of a particular genus. Specific species with different hardiness zone ranges are identified in the Recommended section of each entry. The Quick Reference Chart (pp. 214–217) summarizes different features of the fruit plants.

Each entry gives clear instructions and tips for seeding, planting and growing, and recommends some of our favourite species and varieties. Many more hybrids, cultivars and varieties are often available than we have space to mention. Check with local greenhouses or garden centres when making your selection. That said, we present enough wonderful fruits and berries in this book to provide you with many seasons of gardening pleasure.

Problems and pests that commonly affect fruits and berries are also listed for each entry. Consult the Pests and Diseases section of the Introduction (pp. 65–80) for more information.

Finally, we have tried to avoid jargon, but check the glossary (pp. 218–219) for any unfamiliar terms.

The Fruits
&Berries

Almond • Apricot
Prunus

Features: rounded to spreading, medium, deciduous tree; white or pink, spring flowers; edible fruit or nuts **Height:** 7.5–9 m (25–30') **Spread:** 7.5–9 m (25–30') **Hardiness:** zones 5–8

The tendency for spring frosts to kill flowers and reduce fruit set makes these trees inappropriate for commercial cultivation in most of Canada. But for the backyard orchard, these are pretty trees that will produce fruit or nuts, if somewhat inconsistently.

Growing

Almonds, apricots and their hybrids grow best in **full sun**. The soil should be of **average fertility, neutral to acidic, moist** and **well drained**. Choose a **sheltered** location that is protected from spring frosts. Dwarf selections can be grown in containers. Protect container specimens from winter cold by moving them to a cold but sheltered location such as a shed or unheated garage for winter.

These plants need very little pruning, but dead, damaged and awkward growth can be removed once flowering is complete in spring. They can also be trained as espalier specimens or bonsai.

Tips

When purchasing almond or apricot plants, look for hardy, late-blooming, self-pollinating cultivars. You might

P. armeniaca 'Moongold'

want to consider dwarf plants if you have limited space or would like to grow them in containers.

Harvesting

Pick apricots as soon as they are ripe. They can be eaten fresh, dried or used in jams and preserves. The nuts of almonds and sweet nut apricots should be removed from the fleshy outer layer and dried for storage. They can be eaten raw or roasted.

Recommended

P. armeniaca (apricot) is a small, rounded, deciduous tree that bears pink or white flowers in early spring. It grows up to 9 m (30') tall, with an equal or slightly lesser spread. The small, soft-skinned fruits ripen in midsummer.

P. dulcis (almond, sweet almond) is an open, spreading, deciduous tree that bears pink or white flowers in early spring. The fruits are hard and green with a fuzzy skin. It grows about 7.5 m (25') tall, with an equal spread.

Problems & Pests

Possible problems include aphids, borers, caterpillars, leafhoppers, mites, nematodes, scale insects, canker, crown gall, fire blight, powdery mildew and viruses. Root rot can occur in poorly drained soil. Plants grown in stress-free locations are less likely to suffer serious problems.

Closely related plants in the genus Prunus *tend to cross breed, resulting in several hybrids that have the positive traits of both parents. Several apricot almond cultivars (called sweet nut apricots) with edible nuts are available, as are several almond peach cultivars with edible nuts and a later blooming period.*

P. armeniaca 'Harcot'

Apple

Malus

Features: rounded, mounded or spreading, short to tall, deciduous tree; white, pink or purple, spring flowers; edible fruit in late summer or autumn; autumn colour; attractive habit and bark **Height:** 2–15 m (7–50') **Spread:** 1–15 m (3–50') **Hardiness:** zones 3–8

*I*s the apple not the most familiar and homey of fruits? Apple pie, apple jelly, apples fresh off the tree, apple cider, apple vinegar… The list goes on! With the advent of readily available dwarf stock, an apple tree of one's own is entirely possible for even the smallest home garden.

Growing

Apples grow best in **full sun** but tolerate partial shade with some reduction in fruiting. Choose a **sheltered** location because cold winds can damage flowers in spring, reducing fruit set. The soil should be **average to fertile, slightly acidic, moist** and **well drained**. Plants perform poorly in excessively sandy, rocky or alkaline soils. Clay soils are tolerated as long as they do not stay wet for extended periods of time. Fruiting may be delayed in wet soils that take a long time to warm up in spring. Plant new trees in spring once the soil has warmed.

Apple trees don't actually need to be pruned, but fruit production and even ripening can be greatly improved through good pruning practices.

M. 'McIntosh'

Tips

Apples have been developed and rated for many desirable traits in both the tree and the fruit. Trees can be bred for qualities such as plant size, disease resistance, abundance of fruit and cold hardiness. Fruit may be soft or firm when cooked, sweet or tart to the taste, long-lasting for storage or shorter-lasting for quick eating, and early- or late-ripening. Your best bet is to select disease-resistant plants with the traits you are most interested in and that will grow best in your area.

Harvesting

Apples ripen from late summer to late autumn, depending on variety and climatic conditions.

Recommended

M. x *domestica* is a variable group of hybrids that range in habit from columnar to open and spreading. A recent variety is '**Ambrosia**,' discovered in BC's Similkameen Valley in the 1980s. It's considered hardy with a crisp-fleshed fruit with low acidity. '**Cortland**' is an older variety of dessert apple with a somewhat squat

M. 'Cortland'

shape and very white flesh. '**Empire**' is known for its deep, almost maroon skin and doesn't bruise easily. '**Gala**' is an elegant dessert apple with a pronounced sweetness and is a good candidate for storage. '**McIntosh**,' the quintessential Canadian apple, has good colour and a crunchy bite when fresh. '**Northern Spy**,' an old-fashioned favourite native to the eastern U.S., matures in mid- to late autumn and is often used for pies and cider. '**Spartan**,' another Canadian star, is the first apple developed within a formal scientific breeding program. If you can't decide, it is possible to purchase stock with several varieties of apples grafted onto a single tree.

Crabapple espalier

M. 'Spartan' (above)

The home garden or orchard offers an excellent opportunity to plant and preserve some of our vanishing heritage varieties of apples, such as the 16th-century **'Calville Blanc d'Hiver,'** the charmingly-named **'Webster's Pink Meat'** and **'Brown Snout'** or the distinctively coloured **'Winter Banana.'**

Crabapples, with their stunning bursts of pink or white, spring blossoms, are often grown as flowering shrubs, but many also produce edible fruit. The small fruits, once popular for jellies and cinnamon-flavoured pickles, range from marble to golf ball size and are considered

by many people as simply too tedious to pick. Today, crabapples are more often planted as pollinators for larger-fruited commercial apples or, as in the case of the very cold-hardy **M. baccatta** (Siberian crabapple), used as rootstock. These practices have made it difficult to find crabapples for sale. However, tasty and heavy-bearing crabapple nursery stock is still available for the home gardener. **M. 'Dolgo'** grows to 9 m (30') tall, with a spread of 7.5 m (25'), and has an upright, open habit. It features white blossoms and large, brilliant red fruit prized for jelly (zone 3). **M. 'Molten Lava,'** a white-flowered variety, produces copious

amounts of orange-red fruit. It is considered disease resistant and is a good choice for smaller gardens, growing 4.5 m (15') tall with a weeping spread of 4 m (13') (zone 4). **M. 'Prairiefire'** has attractive bark, pink flowers and dark red fruit that remains on the branches well into late autumn. It grows to 6 m (20') tall with an equal spread (zone 4).

Problems & Pests

Birds, aphids, wasps, coddling moths, scab, powdery mildew, canker and rot can cause problems.

The cultivation of apples dates back to at least 6500 BC, and most of the apples we enjoy originate from crosses between M. sylvestris *and* M. pumila, *though many other species have been bred into the line to encourage hardiness and disease resistance.*

Apple trees perform poorly, bearing little or no fruit, when they don't have a sufficient dormant period in winter. This is rarely, if ever, a problem in Canada.

Banana

Musa

Features: upright habit; exotic appearance; summer flowers; late-summer to autumn fruit **Height:** 1.5–3 m (5–10') **Spread:** up to 1.5 m (5') **Hardiness:** tropical perennial grown as a patio specimen or houseplant

*T*he chances of successfully overwintering an edible variety of banana outdoors in Canada are pretty slim. Banana plants do, however, make interesting patio specimens and will live quite happily in a sunny room indoors. If you have the space, they are attractive, and it will feel like quite the accomplishment to harvest your own bananas.

Growing

Although bananas grow best in **full sun**, plants grown indoors for part of the year may suffer leaf scorch if kept in full sun outdoors. These should be grown in light shade or partial shade outdoors and in a bright location but out of hot windows indoors. The soil should be **fertile, humus rich, moist** and **well drained**. A good potting mix will work well.

Cut stems back to ground level once flowering and fruiting has occurred to make room for new growth.

M. acuminata 'Dwarf Cavendish'

Tips

Growing bananas in containers makes it convenient to move them indoors over winter. If you don't mind some digging in autumn or starting new plants each year, you can plant them directly into a border in your garden.

Harvesting

Bananas develop in large bunches on pendant stems. They will be bright yellow when ripe. The plant stem will die back once it has flowered. Don't despair; more stems should develop.

Recommended

M. acuminata is a variable, upright, suckering perennial with large, bright green to blue-green, paddle-shaped leaves. It bears white or yellow flowers in summer, followed by fruit that ripens to yellow. **'Dwarf Cavendish'** (*M.* x *paradisiaca* 'Dwarf Cavendish') grows only 1.5 m (5') tall, making it more suitable for patio and indoor cultivation.

Problems & Pests

Spider mites, aphids, mealybugs, nematodes, cucumber mosaic virus, anthracnose and wilt can cause problems.

Whatever selection you choose or find, be sure it is an edible variety. Many species have unpalatable fruit.

M. acuminata

Bayberry

Myrica

Features: aromatic, deciduous to semi-evergreen shrub; attractive foliage; dense, suckering habit; persistent fruit **Height:** 1.5–3.6 m (5–12') **Spread:** 1.5–3.6 m (5–12') **Hardiness:** zones 3–6

*A*lthough not edible, the fruit of this shrub is fragrant and popular for use in candles and potpourri.

Growing

Bayberry grows well in **full sun** or **partial shade**. It adapts to most soil conditions, from poor sandy soil to

heavy clay soil. This plant tolerates salty conditions, making it useful where coastal conditions or winter road spray may kill less tolerant plants. Bayberry rarely needs any pruning.

Tips

This adaptable plant forms large colonies and is often spread by birds. Its shiny, semi-evergreen foliage is quite handsome in mass plantings in areas of poor soil and in seaside gardens.

Harvesting

The fruit ripens in autumn and persists all winter. The fragrant wax can be rendered by simmering the fruit in water. The wax will rise to the surface and can be skimmed off.

Recommended

M. pensylvanica is a dense, rounded, suckering shrub that bears insignificant flowers in early to mid-spring. Male and female flowers are generally produced on separate plants, but sometimes the plants are monoecious. Both male and female plants are required for a good show of fruit on the female. Small, waxy, grey fruit persists through winter.

Problems & Pests

Problems with leaf spot, stem rot, root rot, dieback and rust can occur.

The waxy fruit of this eastern North American native has long been used in legendary candle making. Bouquets make lovely winter decorations, especially at holiday time.

Beech

Fagus

Features: large, oval, deciduous shade tree; attractive summer and autumn foliage; smooth, grey bark; edible nuts **Height:** 15–25 m (50–80') **Spread:** 10–20 m (33–65') **Hardiness:** zones 4–8

*B*eech nuts are popular in Europe, though not so much in North America.

Growing

Beeches grow equally well in **full sun** or **partial shade**. The soil should be of **average fertility, acidic, loamy** and **well drained**, though almost all well-drained soils are tolerated.

Very little pruning is required. Remove dead or damaged branches in spring or any time after the damage occurs. European beech is a popular hedging plant that responds well to severe pruning.

Tips

Beeches make excellent specimen trees. They are also used as street trees and shade trees, or in woodland gardens. These trees need a lot of space. European beech's adaptability to pruning makes it a good choice for a small garden.

Harvesting

The nuts ripen in autumn and are edible when roasted.

Recommended

F. sylvatica (European beech) is a spectacular tree that can grow 18 m (60') tall and wide or even larger. It

transplants easily and tolerates varied soil conditions better than American beech. You can find a number of interesting cultivars, and several are small enough to use in the home garden. **'Fastigiata'** ('Dawyck') is a narrow, upright tree. It can grow to 25 m (80') tall, but spreads only about 3 m (10'). Yellow- or purple-leaved forms are available. **'Pendula'** (weeping beech) is a dramatic tree whose pendulous branches reach down to the ground. It varies in form; some spread widely, resulting in a cascade effect, while other specimens may be rather upright, with branches drooping from the central trunk. This cultivar can grow as tall as the species, but a specimen with the branches drooping from the central trunk may be narrow enough for a home garden.

F. sylvatica 'Pendula Purpurea'

Problems & Pests

Canker, powdery mildew, leaf spot, bark disease, borers, scale insects and aphids can afflict beech trees. None of these pests cause serious problems.

Beech nuts provide food for a wide variety of animals, including squirrels and birds, and they were a favourite food of the extinct passenger pigeon.

F. sylvatica 'Pendula'

Blueberry • Cranberry • Huckleberry

Vaccinium

Features: attractive shrub; small, bell-shaped, white or pink flowers; edible fruit; bright red autumn colour **Height:** 10 cm–1.5 m (4"–5') **Spread:** 30 cm–1.5 m (1–5') **Hardiness:** zones 2–9

*T*hese attractive bushes are low and spreading or rounded and upright. The leaves turn a beautiful shade of red in autumn. These plants are an admirable addition to any border, with the added asset of delicious summer fruit.

Growing

These berries grow well in **full sun, partial shade** or **light shade**. The soil should be of **average fertility, acidic, moist** and **well drained**. They grow best in areas where the soil is acidic and peaty or sandy. Soil can be amended, but plants never grow as well in alkaline soil. Cranberries tolerate moist soil. Little pruning is required.

Tips

If you have naturally acidic soil, blueberries make an excellent choice for a fruit-bearing shrub in a woody or mixed border. They are hardy in many Canadian gardens and make interesting low hedges.

Huckleberries also do well in a woody or mixed border. Include them in the vegetable garden or

V. corymbosum 'Bluecrop'

grow them on top of old cedar stumps for a natural look.

Harvesting

Blueberries are ready for harvesting when they turn, not surprisingly, blue. Test one, and if it is sweet and tastes the way you expect, they are ready for harvest.

Cranberries are ripe when they turn bright red.

Harvest huckleberries in early autumn when the foliage above the berries turns brown and begins to curl and the berries are dark and soft to the touch.

Recommended

V. angustifolium var. *laevifolium* (lowbush blueberry, wild blueberry) is a low, bushy, spreading shrub with small, glossy, green leaves that turn red in autumn. It grows 10–60 cm (4–24") tall and spreads 30–60 cm (12–24"). Clusters of small, bell-shaped, white or pink flowers are produced in spring, followed by

V. corymbosum

small, round fruit that ripens to dark blue in midsummer. (Zones 2–8)

V. corymbosum (highbush blueberry) is a bushy, upright, arching shrub with green leaves that turn red or yellow in autumn. It grows 90 cm–1.5 m (3–5') tall with an equal spread. Clusters of white or pink flowers at the ends of the branches in spring are followed by berries that ripen to bright blue in summer. Several cultivars are available, including **'Bluecrop,'** with tart, light blue berries; **'Blueray,'** with large, dark blue berries; and **'Chippewa,'** with sweet, light blue berries. (Zones 3–8)

V. macrocarpon (cranberry) is a low-growing, evergreen shrub with dark green leaves that turn bright red to bronze in autumn and winter. Bell-shaped, pink flowers are followed by bright red fruit. (Zones 2–7)

V. ovatum (evergreen huckleberry) is a west coast native. It is a compact, bushy, evergreen shrub that grows 90 cm–3.6 m (3–12') tall and spreads 1.5–3 m (5–10'). Small, red or pink flowers in late spring or early summer are followed by edible, dark blue berries in early autumn. Berries can remain on the bush until December, and some people say they taste better after the first frost. (Zones 7–9)

V. parvifolium (red huckleberry, deciduous huckleberry) is native to the Pacific Northwest. It is an upright, bushy, mainly deciduous

V. vitis-idaea (above)
V. angustifolium (below)

shrub that grows to 3 m (10') tall and spreads to 1.8 m (6'). Small, white or pink flowers appear in late spring and early summer, followed by edible, bright red berries. (Zones 5–8)

V. vitis-idaea (bog cranberry, lingonberry) is native to the arctic and boreal regions of North America. It is a low-growing, spreading, evergreen shrub, growing to 25 cm (10") tall with an indefinite spread. This species tolerates wet soils. It bears white or pink flowers in late spring and early summer, followed by edible, red berries. Although it tolerates extremely severe winters without difficulty, it is less tolerant of summer heat and is best reserved for gardens in the colder areas of Canada. **Var.** *minimus* is a smaller and even hardier variety, growing to 20 cm (8") tall. (Zones 2–6)

Problems & Pests

Rare problems with caterpillars, rust, scale, powdery mildew and root rot can occur.

A handy way to preserve blueberries is to spread them on a cookie sheet and put them in the freezer. Once they are frozen, they can be put into an air-tight bag and kept in the freezer. The berries will be frozen individually, rather than in a solid block, making it easy to measure out just what you need for a single recipe or serving.

V. parvifolium

Cape Gooseberry
Ground Cherry
Physalis

Features: trailing or creeping plant much like a tomato; yellow, blue or white, small flowers; edible and ornamental fruit **Height:** 1 m (3') **Spread:** 1 m (3') **Hardiness:** annual; tender perennial grown as an annual

Cape gooseberry got its name in the early 19th century when the small, juicy, golden fruit, with its crisp, paper-like husk, was exported from the Cape of Good Hope. The pricey and uncommon fruit is now more likely to be shipped from New Zealand or China.

Growing

Cape gooseberries do best in **full sun**. Light shade is tolerated with somewhat reduced fruiting. The soil should be of **average fertility, moist** and **well drained**. For best results, start plants indoors as you would tomatoes. Plants need a long, warm growing season to develop colour. Pinch out new shoots to encourage bushy growth.

Tips

Cape gooseberries grow well in pots, especially the small *P. pruinosa* varieties. Cape gooseberries can also be included in the vegetable garden or a naturalistic border where their rustic, casual appearance will be appreciated.

P. peruviana

Harvesting

The papery husk that surrounds each fruit turns beige or light brown when the fruit is ripe. Fruit in the husk can be stored for up to three months.

Recommended

P. pruinosa (dwarf cape gooseberry) is an annual with hairy stems and hairy calyxes. **'Aunt Molly,'** developed in Poland, has good flavour for eating fresh or making jam. **'Little Lantern'** is an especially small, compact plant with a spreading habit. Its dull yellow berries are often described as tasting slightly like pineapple.

P. peruviana is a tender, tropical perennial with a brighter yellow berry encased in a long, pointed calyx. **'Golden Berry'** produces rich-tasting fruit. **'Giant Poha Berry'** grows 30–75 cm (12–30") tall and has fuzzy, sage-coloured leaves.

Problems & Pests

If flea beetles are a problem, try crop row covers.

*Physalis, a member of the nightshade family, includes the tomatillo (*P. ixocarpa*) and the familiar Chinese lantern plant (*P. alkekengi), with its decorative orange husks.*

Cherry

Prunus

Features: upright, rounded, spreading or weeping, deciduous tree or shrub; spring to early-summer flowers; edible fruit; attractive bark; colourful autumn foliage
Height: 1.5–18 m (5–60') **Spread:** 1.5–10 m (5–33') **Hardiness:** zones 2–8

Like many other fruits, cherries have the best flavour when picked fresh compared to store-bought. The sweet cherries are not hardy in many parts of Canada, but several of the tart or sour cherries are.

Growing

Cherries grow best in **full sun**. The soil should be of **average fertility, moist** and **well drained**. Shallow roots will emerge from the ground if the tree is not getting sufficient water.

In general, two different cultivars of sweet cherries that bloom at the same time are needed for pollination to occur, though there are a few self-fertile cultivars available.

Pruning should be done after flowering. Remove damaged growth and wayward branches as required.

Tips

Prunus species are beautiful as specimen plants, and many are small enough to be included in almost any

garden. Small species and cultivars can also be included in borders or grouped to form informal hedges or barriers.

Among other things, gardeners have used nets, cages, motion deterrents and hot pepper sauce to keep birds off their cherry trees.

Harvesting

Cherries ripen from midsummer to autumn, depending on the variety. The birds will begin to snack on them before they are quite ripe enough for you to pick. The fruits, but not the pits, are edible.

Recommended

P. avium (sweet cherry) is an upright, deciduous tree with red bark and dark green leaves that turn red or yellow in autumn. Clusters of white flowers in spring are followed

P. tomentosa (above)

by bright red fruit in mid- to late summer. It can grow to 18 m (60') tall, with a spread half that much. This is the species from which most of the sweet cherry cultivars have been developed. **'Bing'** is a well-known sweet cherry. **'Stella'** was the first self-fertile sweet cherry to be developed.

P. cerasus (sour cherry) is a rounded, spreading, deciduous tree. Clusters of white, spring flowers are followed by bright red fruit. It grows about 4 m (13') tall, with up to an equal spread. **'Montmorency'** is a popular cultivar.

P. x **'Evans'** (Evans cherry) is a hardy sour cherry of uncertain parentage. It has an upright, arching or spreading habit. It grows 3–4.5 m (10–15') tall, with up to an equal spread.

P. maackii (Amur chokecherry) is a rounded tree that grows 9–14 m (30–45') tall and spreads 7.5–14 m (25–45'). It tolerates cold winter weather. Fragrant, white, mid-spring flowers are followed by red fruits that ripen to black. The glossy, peeling bark is reddish or golden brown and provides interest in the garden all year. (Zones 2–6)

P. tomentosa (Nanking cherry) is a dense, spreading shrub with slightly hairy, serrated foliage.

P. avium 'Sweet Stella'

White or pinkish, spring flowers are followed by red fruit that ripens in late summer or autumn. It grows 2–3 m (7–10') tall and spreads to 5 m (16'). (Zones 2–7)

Problems & Pests

The many possible problems include aphids, borers, caterpillars, leafhoppers, mites, nematodes, scale insects, canker, crown gall, fire blight, powdery mildew and viruses. Root rot can occur in poorly drained soils. Stress-free plants are less likely to have problems.

Although most cherries have edible flesh, the pits, bark and leaves contain hydrocyanic acid and are toxic.

P. tomentosa (above)
P. avium (below)

Chestnut
Castanea

Features: vigorous, deciduous tree or large shrub; bold, dark green foliage; summer flowers; edible nuts **Height:** 6–30 m (20–100') **Spread:** 1.5–21 m (5–70') **Hardiness:** zones 4–9

*T*he American chestnut (*C. dentata*) once dominated the eastern hardwood forests of North America. In 1906, chestnut blight was introduced to North America, where it quickly and almost completely wiped these trees out. Breeding programs have been working for years to breed disease resistance into the species with the hope that the tree can be reintroduced to reclaim its majestic position.

Growing

Chestnuts grow well in **full sun** or **light shade**. The soil should be **average to fertile, slightly acidic, deep, moist** and **well drained**.

Remove dead or damaged growth as needed, and prune lightly to shape the trees in spring.

Tips

These trees are generally a bit too big for the average home garden. Chinquapin chestnut is a smaller species, but it can be susceptible to chestnut blight.

Harvesting

The nuts ripen in autumn. They are edible once roasted.

Recommended

C. mollissima (Chinese chestnut) is a large, spreading tree with deeply furrowed mature bark. It grows up to 21 m (70') tall, with an equal spread. Cream-coloured, summer flowers are followed by spiny-hulled nuts in autumn. (Zones 4–8)

C. pumila (chinquapin) is a large shrub or small tree. It grows 6–8 m (20–25') tall and spreads 1.5–2.4 m

(5–8'). Cream-coloured flowers in summer are followed by edible nuts in autumn. This tree attracts wildlife. (Zones 5–9)

C. sativa (sweet chestnut, Spanish chestnut) is a large, columnar tree. It grows up to 30 m (100') tall and spreads 15 m (50'). Cream-coloured flowers are followed by edible, autumn nuts. Several named cultivars, such as **'Marron de Lyon,'** have been developed for their improved nut production. (Zones 4–8)

Problems & Pests

Chestnut blight, dieback, stem canker, heart rot, powdery mildew, fungal blight and leaf scorch can be problems.

A paper sack of hot, roasted chestnuts is a delightful treat on a chilly, late-autumn evening during the hectic holiday shopping season. Candied chestnuts (marrons glacés) are also a star ingredient in many classic European desserts.

Chokeberry

Aronia

Features: suckering, deciduous shrub; spring flowers; bitter fruit; autumn foliage
Height: 1–1.8 m (3–6') **Spread:** 1–3 m (3–10') **Hardiness:** zones 3–8

*A*lthough considered very bitter, the fruit of chokeberry is rich in vitamin C and is used in Europe for the juice. If you find the fruit too unpalatable to eat, then simply enjoy this shrub for its ornamental qualities.

Growing

Chokeberries grow well in **full sun** or **partial shade**, but the best flowering and fruiting occurs in full sun. The soil should be of **average fertility** and **well drained**, but plants adapt to most soils and tolerate wet or dry soil and poor soil.

Up to one-third of the older stems can be pruned out annually once flowering is finished.

Tips

These plants can be naturalized or planted in a shrub or mixed border. They can even make interesting low-maintenance specimen plants. They are a good choice for parts of the garden that you only get to every now and again. Left to their own devices, they will eventually colonize a fairly large area.

The berries will persist all winter, so there is no rush to pick them.

A. melanocarpa

Harvesting

It is best to harvest these berries after they've had at least a couple of good frosts because the cold reduces some of the bitterness. The best way to prepare them is to combine them with other fruit when making jellies.

Recommended

A. melanocarpa (black chokeberry) is an upright, suckering shrub native to eastern North America. It grows 1–1.8 m (3–6') tall and can spread to about 3 m (10'). It bears white flowers in late spring and early summer, followed by dark fruit that ripens in autumn and persists through winter. Foliage turns bright red to purplish red in autumn. **'Autumn Magic'** bears larger, shinier fruit and has excellent autumn colour. **'Iroquois Beauty'** ('Morton') is a compact cultivar developed at the Morton Arboretum. It grows only 1 m (3') tall. **'Viking'** has glossy, dark green foliage that turns dark red in autumn. It

'Iroquois Beauty'

grows 1–1.5 m (3–5') tall. The persistent, dark fruit is edible, but bitter.

Problems & Pests

They rarely suffer from any major problems, though some fungal leaf spot or rust is possible.

'Autumn Magic'

Citrus

Citrus

Features: bushy, spiny, usually evergreen shrub or tree; fragrant flowers; often edible fruit **Height:** 60 cm–2.4 m (2–8') in containers **Spread:** 60 cm–1.2 m (2–4') in containers **Hardiness:** tender; grown as a bonsai, patio specimen or indoor plant

Lemons, limes, oranges, grapefruits and tangelos (a cross between tangerine and grapefruit) are all members of the colourful citrus family. With their bright skins and lively flavour, citrus fruits are a welcome addition to any meal. The glossy, evergreen leaves and fragrant blossoms are a delight in the garden or, more likely for Canadians, the greenhouse or sunroom.

Growing

Citrus trees prefer **full sun**, but plants grown indoors for part of the year may suffer leaf scorch if kept in full sun outdoors. These should be grown in light shade or partial shade outdoors and in a bright location but out of hot windows indoors. The soil should be of **average fertility, moist** and **well drained.**

Most citrus trees will tolerate light frost but should still be brought indoors before the first frost.

Tips

Citrus trees are attractive specimens, but unless you have a solarium or very sunny location indoors, most will rarely, if ever, bear fruit. Several dwarf cultivars have been developed, and many avid indoor citrus growers have had great success with these.

Citrus trees are dependable and attractive patio specimens and houseplants. Keep in mind that most of them get quite large, even in a container, and that almost all have spiny barbs at the leaf axils.

C. sinensis 'Valencia' (above)
C. limon (below)

Citrus trees are also popular for their use as bonsai; some of the most interesting bonsai specimens are oranges. A tiny, distorted plant bearing a large, ripe orange seems oddly yet interestingly incongruous.

Harvesting

Pick the fruit as soon as it is ripe. Makrut lime is grown for the leaves as well as the fruit. They are frequently used as a flavouring ingredient in Thai cooking, and gourmet cooks may enjoy having a fresh supply readily available.

Recommended

There are many species of citrus available. They will grow to be small, bushy trees in containers and often have fragrant foliage. If they do

C. limon (above)
C. limon 'Meyeri' (below)

flower and fruit, the flowers are wonderfully fragrant, and the flowers and fruit will often develop contiguously. You can often sprout a plant from the seeds found within purchased fruit. A few to consider are *C. aurantifolia* (lime), *C. aurantium* (bitter or Seville orange), *C. hystrix* (makrut lime, kaffir lime), *C. limon* (lemon), *C. limon* 'Meyeri' (dwarf lemon, Meyer lemon), *C. paradisi* (grapefruit), *C. reticulata* (Mandarin, Clementine, tangerine) and *C. sinensis* (sweet orange).

Problems & Pests

Several rot and fungal problems can occur, and scale insects, nematodes, plant bugs, weevils, aphids, mealybugs, spider mites and whiteflies can also cause problems.

C. limon

There are some inedible selections of citrus available as houseplants that will flower and fruit more dependably than the recommended fruit species if you are more interested in an ornamental citrus plant.

C. sinensis

Currant • Gooseberry

Ribes

Features: shrub with long, arching, sometimes prickly stems; attractive lobed leaves; yellow, pink or red, often fragrant flowers; edible fruit **Height:** 45 cm–3 m (18"–10') **Spread:** 45 cm–2.4 m (18"–8') **Hardiness:** zones 3–8

Gooseberry produces a tart fruit that varies from pale green to yellow to pinkish purple when fully ripe. Currants are equally varied, available in red, white and black. Both berries, mainstays in colonial cookery, are making a comeback in the "current" (sorry!) trend toward local-harvest, seasonal cuisine.

Growing

Currants and gooseberries grow and fruit best in **full sun**, but they don't mind some shade from intense afternoon heat. The soil should be **average to fertile, moist** and **well drained**. These long-lived shrubs will survive a considerable amount of neglect, but for good berry production, site both currants and gooseberries in areas with access to regular maintenance along with shelter from the wind.

When planting, dig a hole of sufficient volume to allow the roots to be fully extended. Be careful to set the plant at its previous soil mark. A thick mulch helps maintain cool roots. Weed carefully to avoid damaging the relatively shallow roots. Annual pruning is a good idea; cut away old wood at ground level.

R. nigrum

Tips

Currants, with their attractively coloured berries—red, soft yellow or rich black—can be included in a woody mixed border or added to the vegetable garden.

The gooseberry, with its inconspicuous blossoms and green fruits, tends to blend into surrounding vegetation and is often unfairly relegated to a forgotten corner of the backyard.

Harvesting

Berries ripen in mid- to late summer but will require several pickings because they do not ripen all at the same time. Gooseberries can be stripped from the branch with a gloved hand and the debris winnowed later. For ease of picking, gather currants in clusters, not individually. A fork, used gently, makes a great tool for later stripping the clusters. Berries will keep several days in the fridge (gooseberries often last for up to two weeks) and also make wonderful preserves and jams.

Recommended

R. nigrum (black currant) grows to 1.5 m (5') tall with an equal spread and has fragrant foliage and glossy, black berries. It is not quite as long-lived as red or white currants. The dwarf **'Ben Sarek'** is both prolific and mildew-resistant, and the Canadian-developed varieties **'Consort,' 'Coronet'** and **'Crusader'** are considered blister-rust resistant.

R. rubrum (red currant, white currant) grows 90 cm–1.8 m (3–6') tall, with a 60 cm–1.5 m (2–5') spread, and has small berries, with the colour depending on the variety. **'Jonkheer van Tets,'** an early variety

of red currant cultivated commercially in the Netherlands, is mildew resistant. **'Red Lake'** is more flavourful and produces large, red berries. The white currant **'White Imperial'** is a small, upright shrub. The larger **'White Versailles'** produces sweet, pale yellow fruit. Many cooks consider the grape-flavoured white currant tastier than the milder red currant.

R. uva-crispa (gooseberry) fruits best in areas that are likely to experience frost, which Canada has no shortage of. **'Invicta'** bears a heavy crop of large fruit. **'Pixwell'** is a hardy variety with shorter thorns than most, with the advantage that the fruit tends to hang away from the thorns.

Problems & Pests

Birds, aphids, mildew, blight and rust are potential problems. Currants, especially black currant, and gooseberry are often implicated in white pine blister rust. The rust requires both the pine and a *Ribes* species to complete its life cycle. The disease does little harm to the berry bush but is lethal to the pine. If you garden in a white pine area, certain varieties of currant and gooseberry may be prohibited.

Currants and gooseberries shine in northern climates, enjoying, as they do, a good dose of frost and winter cold for the best fruit production.

Elderberry
Elder
Sambucus

Features: large, bushy, deciduous shrub; early-summer flowers; fruit; foliage
Height: 1.5–6 m (5–20') **Spread:** 1.5–6 m (5–20') **Hardiness:** zones 3–8

*E*lderberry is very hardy, tolerates most soil conditions and requires little care. It can, in fact, be a little too easy to grow; it has a tendency to spread, either by seed or sucker. With its creamy flowers and clusters of smoky purple berries, though, it can be an attractive addition to the wilder parts of the garden.

Growing

Elders grow well in **full sun** or **partial shade**. The soil should be of **average fertility, moist** and **well drained**. These plants tolerate dry soil once established.

With its suckering habit, elderberry can look untidy without regular pruning.

Tips

Elders can be used in a shrub or mixed border, in a natural woodland garden or next to a pond or other water feature.

The raw berries are marginally edible but not palatable and can cause stomach upset, particularly in children. All other parts of elders are toxic.

Harvesting

Berries are harvested in early autumn and are easy to pick from the upright, thornless shrub. At this point they can be frozen and brought out later in winter, when the busy harvest season is over, to make into preserves or pies.

Recommended

S. canadensis (sweet elder, American elder) is a deciduous, hardy shrub growing 1.5–3 m (5–10') tall with a similar spread and is the preferred choice for berries. Sprays of tiny, white, star-like flowers are followed by clusters of small, purply black berries. Two popular varieties are **'New York 21,'** a productive hybrid, and **'York,'** a large bush with good-size fruit. 'York' bears best with cross-pollination with another cultivar.

S. nigra (European elder, black elder) is a rounded shrub with white flowers followed by dark purple ber-

S. canadensis

ries. It grows 6 m (20') tall and spreads 4.5 m (15'). **'Aurea'** has fragrant flowers and yellow leaves.

Problems & Pests

These plants are pretty much pest-free, except for a little competition from birds.

S. canadensis

Fig
Ficus

Features: bush-like tree; bulbous, velvety, green or purple fruits **Height:** 1.8–4.5 m (6–15') **Spread:** up to 4 m (13') **Hardiness:** zones 7–10

Ficus includes at least 800 species, most of which are grown for shade or for their attractive foliage.

Growing

Figs are semi-tropical and should be planted in **full sun** in a **sheltered** spot, ideally facing south against a building. The soil should be **deep, rich, moist** and **well drained**. Avoid over-fertilizing to prevent rapid new growth that can be damaged by cold.

Provide thick mulch in winter and be prepared for die-back at the top of the plant. For additional winter protection, tie the stems together, surround them with a wire cage filled with leaves and wrap everything with a waterproof covering. Prune dead and damaged branches to keep the plant healthy.

Tips

Figs usually bear two crops, with the second harvest considerably lighter. Many varieties of figs bear fruit on both old wood and new shoots. Raising them in pots may allow you to shelter the plants and extend the growing season enough to allow you to harvest fruit from the new shoots.

FIG 121

Harvesting

Leave figs on the tree until they are ripe enough to drop from their own weight. If birds are a problem, try tying a paper bag around the fruit. If you don't polish them off fresh, the succulent fruits can be preserved or dried.

Recommended

F. carica (common fig, edible fig) is the species that bears edible fruit and is one of the oldest cultivated crops. Most varieties are self-pollinating. '**Adriatic**' bears fruit on both old and new wood and does well in cool coastal regions. '**Brown Turkey**' is a productive and reliable choice. '**King**' is an especially sweet variety that sets fruit on older wood, so prune selectively. '**Negronne**,' a dwarf variety that grows 1.8–2.4 m (6–8') tall, is suited to small gardens.

Problems & Pests

The fig has been with us for hundreds of years and is relatively pest and disease free. Rain can split ripening fruit. Birds and wasps, which recognize a good thing, may want a share of the fruit.

F. carica

Despite modern transportation, fresh figs are a rare treat in markets and are worth the winter precautions to have an ample supply in summer.

Ginkgo
Ginkgo

Features: deciduous tree that is conical in youth and variable with age; summer and autumn foliage; fruit; bark **Height:** 9–30 m (30–100') **Spread:** 3–30 m (10–100') **Hardiness:** zones 3–9

Most of us in Canada grow these trees for their attractive habit and foliage, but the nuts are an important commercial crop in many Asian countries. Only the female trees provide nuts. However, the fruit that surrounds the nut smells unpleasant, so a female plant can be difficult to come by in a standard nursery. Female selections can usually be ordered from specialty growers.

Growing

Ginkgo prefers **full sun**. The soil should be **fertile, sandy** and **well drained,** but this tree adapts to most conditions. It also tolerates urban conditions and cold weather.

If you desire the nuts, remember you need a male tree for fertilization and a female tree to bear the fruit. Little or no pruning is necessary.

Tips

These pollution-tolerant trees are good choices for city gardens. Although they grow very slowly, ginkgos eventually become very large and are best suited as specimens in parks and large gardens. They can also be used as street trees.

Harvesting

Be patient. A female ginkgo is at least 20 years old before it begins to produce nuts. Collect the nuts when they drop from the tree in late summer and autumn.

Recommended
G. biloba has existed for 150 million years. As it matures, its arresting shape can vary from gently cascading to wildly erratic. Although it is a slow starter, sometimes taking 10 to 12 years to get going, it is well worth the wait. In autumn, the matte green, fan-shaped leaves turn a glorious golden yellow.

Female trees drop fleshy, unpleasant-smelling, yellow-brown fruits containing an edible, almond-shaped kernel. **'Geisha,'** a new trademarked introduction from Japan, is a heavy fruit producer. **'Salem Lady,'** selected in Salem, Oregon, also yields good quantities of thin-shelled nuts.

There is a greater selection of male varieties to choose from because they are much more popular, especially for landscape use, than females. **'Fastigiata'** is a slender cultivar reaching 9 m (30') tall. **'Male'** is considered a good pollinator. **'Princeton Sentry'** is narrow and upright, growing 15–25 m (50–80') tall with a 7.5 m (25') spread.

Problems & Pests
This tree seems to have outlived most of the pests that might have afflicted it. Leaf spot may affect ginkgo, but it doesn't cause any real trouble.

Ginkgo appears to have been saved from extinction by its long-time use in Asian temple gardens. Today, this "living fossil" grows almost entirely in horticultural settings.

Goji Berry
Wolfberry
Lycium

Features: spiny shrub forming a dense thicket of arching branches; white and mauve, trumpet-like flowers; orange-red, autumn berries **Height:** 1–4 m (3–13') **Spread:** 1–2.5 m (3–8') **Hardiness:** zones 4–9

Goji, touted for its health properties and long history in traditional Chinese medicine, is advertised as reputedly benefiting a list of ailments including arthritis, diabetes, heart disease and cancer. The seedy, grape-size berries are said to have slight overtones of tomato and taste somewhat like a sweet cranberry. Goji is available dried and, more often, as juice.

Growing

Goji prefers **full sun**. For best fruiting results, a full eight hours of sunlight is recommended. The soil should be **rich** with lots of organic matter, **moist** and **well drained**. Use a shallow mulch, and water in the early morning, avoiding wetting the leaves.

Seeds and plants are available from at least one Canadian mail order seed company. The adventuresome grower can also try germinating seed from dried goji. Plant seeds or plants in pots or directly into the garden in spring.

Tips

Goji is considered an adaptable plant with reports of it surviving freezing temperatures as well as conditions of high heat and humidity.

Harvesting

Flowers set throughout summer, and the berries should be ready to eat by late autumn. Gather berries when they've gone from green to red and have a sweet taste. Shoots and leaves may also be harvested and used as a leafy vegetable.

Recommended

L. chinense (Chinese wolfberry) is sometimes marketed as goji berry. As with any plant or food supplement that's suddenly in the media limelight, there is considerable hype to wade through. Chinese wolfberry is a distant cousin to the true Tibetan goji, and some reports say it should not even be called goji because that designation is only for *L. eleagnus.* However, wolfberry's appearance, habit and growing requirements are the same as for goji, though it may not grow quite as tall. (Zones 5–9)

L. eleagnus barbarum (Tibetan goji, Mongolian goji), often advertised as a Himalayan berry, also grows in China. Both light purple and white, trumpet-shaped flowers begin in summer and continue until frost. The flowers develop into small, oval, red berries containing varying numbers of tiny, yellow seeds. Tibetan goji is a vigorous plant and can reach heights of 3 m (10') over five years if not pruned.

L. europaeum may have a slightly more upright shape than the other two species, but with an almost identical appearance, it is often mistaken for either of the other two species, a typical problem for all three plants. Growing conditions are the same as for goji. (Zones 5–9)

Problems & Pests

Gogi, an ancient plant, appears relatively pest-free. Slugs and deer can take a liking to it, though. Wet leaves may cause fungal problems.

Goji, the current "superfood" darling in the health food supplement spotlight, has not only been cultivated in Asia for centuries but also grown in the United Kingdom since the 1700s.

Grape

Vitis

Features: woody, climbing, deciduous vine; summer and autumn foliage; late-summer to autumn fruit **Height:** 7–15 m (22–50') **Spread:** 7–15 m (22–50')
Hardiness: zones 4–8

We usually think of grape vines only for their fruit, but their fast-growing nature, dense habit and attractive foliage make them ideal for quickly creating privacy barriers and providing shade for porches. Let them do multiple duty in your garden, providing fruit, shade and privacy.

Growing

Grapes produce best in **full sun**, but the plants tolerate partial shade. The soil should be **moist, acidic** and **well drained**. Grapes tolerate most well-drained soil conditions.

Trim grape plants to fit the space you have, in midwinter and again in midsummer. If you wish to train a grape more formally, cut the side shoots back to within two or three buds of the main stems. Such pruning encourages flowering and fruiting.

Tips

Grape vines can be trained to grow up and over almost any sturdy structure. They may need to be tied in place until the basic structure is established. Grow them up walls, over fences, up porch rails, on pergolas or arbours or almost anywhere else.

The ripe fruit can attract wasps. You may wish to avoid planting this vine near the house if any family members are allergic to bee or wasp stings.

Harvesting

The phrase "grape harvest" conjures up romantic images of crisp, autumn days and post-harvest feasts in the vineyard on checkered tablecloths. The harvest is imbued with tradition and a certain mystique but really it's as straightforward as waiting until the grapes are ripe (browning of the stems of the bunches is a good indicator) and then snipping the bunches. Scissors are great for this. Your biggest concern will be watching out for bees or, depending on where you live, feasting bears. If you have a cool, humid cellar, fresh grapes, stored in a single layer, should keep for months.

Inedible members of the grape family include many ornamental climbing vines such as Virginia creeper.

Recommended

V. vinifera (wine grape) is a woody climber best known for the wine grapes it produces. It makes an attractive addition to the garden. It grows up to 7 m (22') tall and bears edible fruit. Check with your local nursery or contact a specialty grower to see what grapes will grow best in your garden.

Problems & Pests

Diseases and pests to watch for include downy mildew, powdery mildew, canker, dieback, grey mould, black rot, root rot, leaf spot, grape leaf skeletonizer, scale insects and

mealybugs. These problems are not likely to be as serious in a garden with only one or two plants as they are in a vineyard.

Although V. vinifera *varieties are the grapes of choice for home and commercial use, uncountable numbers of other edible* Vitis *species have been enjoyed for millennia around the world.*

Grape leaves can be used in cooking, such as in Middle Eastern dolma, for which grape leaves are used as wrappers to contain a savoury rice mixture.

Hawthorn
Crataegus

Features: rounded, deciduous tree, often with a zig-zag, layered branch pattern; late-spring or early-summer flowers; edible fruit; glossy foliage; thorny branches **Height:** 4.5–9 m (15–30') **Spread:** 3.6–9 m (12–30') **Hardiness:** zones 3–8

C. phaenopyrum

Hawthorns are usually grown as ornamental shrubs and trees, but the fruit is edible. It is not exceptionally flavourful, but it can be used to make jams and jellies, perhaps combined with crabapple for zestyness.

Growing

Hawthorns grow equally well in **full sun** or **partial shade**. They adapt to any **well-drained** soil and tolerate urban conditions.

When grown as trees, hawthorns need little pruning. Those grown as hedges can be pruned after flowering or in autumn. Remove any dead or diseased growth immediately to prevent the spread of diseases such as fire blight and rust.

Hawthorns can become weedy, with seedlings and suckers popping up unexpectedly. Remove any that you find while they are small because they become quite tenacious once they get bigger.

Tips

Hawthorns can be grown as specimen plants or hedges in urban sites, coastal gardens and exposed locations. They are popular in areas where vandalism is a problem because very few people wish to grapple with plants bearing stiff, 5 cm (2") long thorns. As a hedge, hawthorns create an almost impenetrable barrier.

These trees are small enough to include in most gardens. With the long, sharp thorns, however, a hawthorn might not be a good selection if there are children about.

Harvesting

The fruit ripens in autumn, but the flavour is improved if the fruit is left until after the first frost before picking.

Recommended

C. laevigata (*C. oxycantha*; English hawthorn) is a low-branching, rounded tree with zig-zag layers of thorny branches. It grows 4.5–7.5 m

C. laevigata 'Paul's Scarlet'

(15–25') tall and spreads 3.6–7.5 m (12–25'). White or pink, late-spring flowers are followed by bright red fruit in late summer. Many cultivars are available. **'Paul's Scarlet'** ('Paulii,' 'Coccinea Plena') has many showy, deep pink, double flowers. (Zones 4–8)

The genus name Crataegus *comes from the Greek word* kratos, *meaning "strength," in reference to the hard, finegrained wood.*

C. laevigata

C. phaenopyrum (*C. cordata*; Washington hawthorn) is an oval to rounded, thorny tree. It grows 7.5–9 m (25–30') tall, with a spread of 6–9 m (20–30'). It bears white flowers from early to midsummer and has persistent, shiny, red fruit in autumn. The glossy, green foliage turns red and orange in autumn. This species is least susceptible to fire blight.

C. laevigata (left)

Problems & Pests

Borers, caterpillars, leaf miners, skel-etonizers, scale insects, fire blight, canker, rust, powdery mildew, scab and fungal leaf spot are all possible problems. Healthy, stress-free plants will be less susceptible.

Hawthorns are members of the rose family, and their fragrant flowers call to mind the scent of apple blossoms.

C. laevigata 'Paul's Scarlet' (above & below)

Hazelnut
Hazel, Filbert
Corylus

Features: large, dense, deciduous shrub or small tree; early-spring catkins; nuts; foliage **Height:** 2.4–6 m (8–20') **Spread:** 3–4.5 m (10–15') **Hardiness:** zones 3–8

*H*azelnut, also known as filbert, is a decorative tree with inconspicuous flowers but showy catkins. Enclosed in a fringed husk, the nuts develop into a charming and distinctive shape.

Growing

Hazels grow equally well in **full sun** or **partial shade**. The soil should be **fertile** and **well drained**.

These plants require very little pruning but tolerate it well.

Tips

Use hazels as specimens or in shrub or mixed borders. A hedge will provide you with both nuts and privacy and will attract birds to your garden.

Harvesting

Collect the nuts in autumn, once they are ripe.

Recommended

C. americana (American filbert) is a large, multi-stemmed shrub. It bears yellow catkins in spring, and the edible nuts ripen in autumn. It grows

3–4.5 m (10–15') tall and spreads up to 4 m (13').

C. avellana (European hazel, European filbert) grows as a large shrub or small tree. It reaches 3.6–6 m (12–20') in height and spreads up to 4.5 m (15'). Male plants bear long, dangling catkins in late winter and early spring, and female plants develop edible nuts in autumn.

Problems & Pests
Powdery mildew, blight, Japanese beetles, canker, fungal leaf spot, rust, bud mites, tent caterpillars and webworm may cause occasional problems.

Forked hazel branches have been used as divining rods to find underground water or precious metals.

C. avellana 'Contorta' (above)

Highbush Cranberry
American Cranberrybush
Viburnum

Features: bushy or spreading, evergreen or deciduous shrub; spring flowers; attractive summer and autumn foliage; edible fruit **Height:** 1.5–4.5 m (5–15') **Spread:** 1.5–3.6 m (5–12') **Hardiness:** zones 2–9

Highbush cranberry, variously called pimbina or pembina, is a member of the varied and prolific viburnum family that includes snowball tree and Korean spice bush.

Little pruning is needed. Remove awkward, dead, damaged or diseased branches as they occur. Fruiting is better when more than one plant of a species and of a different cultivar are grown.

Growing

Highbush cranberries grow well in **full sun, partial shade** or **light shade**. The soil should be of **average fertility, moist** and **well drained**. These plants tolerate both alkaline and acidic soils.

Tips

Highbush cranberries can be used in borders and woodland gardens. They are a good choice for plantings near patios, decks and swimming pools.

Harvesting

Pick the ripe fruit in autumn. It can be sweetened somewhat by freezing or by picking it after the first frost or two.

Recommended

V. trilobum is a dense, rounded, deciduous shrub native to much of central North America. It grows 2.4–4.5 m (8–15') tall and spreads 2.4–3.6 m (8–12'). Early-summer clusters of showy sterile and inconspicuous fertile flowers are followed by edible, red fruit. The autumn colour is red. This species is resistant to aphids. **'Compactum'** is a smaller, denser shrub that grows 1.5–1.8 m (5–6') tall and wide. Its flowers and fruit resemble those of the species, and it is hardy in zones 2–7.

Problems & Pests

Aphids, borers, dieback, downy mildew, grey mould, leaf spot, mealybugs, powdery mildew, scale insects,

treehoppers, *Verticillium* wilt, weevils and wood rot can affect highbush cranberries.

Although cranberry sauce is traditionally made with the fruit of the American cranberry (Vaccinium macrocarpon, *p. 98), the fruit of* Viburnum trilobum *makes an acceptable alternative. The large seeds must be strained out of the highbush cranberry sauce.*

Juniper Berry
Juniperus

Features: evergreen, ovoid or columnar tree, or rounded or spreading shrub; attractive foliage in varied colours; edible fruit **Height:** 45 cm–6 m (18"–20') **Spread:** 1–6 m (3–20') **Hardiness:** zones 2–9

We rarely consider junipers as fruiting plants, but the berries are edible and are used as a flavouring ingredient in a variety of recipes.

Growing

Junipers prefer **full sun** but tolerate light shade. Ideally, the soil should be of **average fertility** and **well drained**, but these plants tolerate most conditions.

Although these evergreens rarely need pruning, they tolerate it well. They can be trimmed in summer as required to maintain their shape or to limit their size.

Tips

With the wide variety of junipers available, there are endless uses for them in the garden. They make prickly barriers and hedges, and they can be used in borders, as specimens or in groups. The larger species can be used to form windbreaks, while the low-growing species can be used in rock gardens and as groundcovers.

Juniper was used traditionally to purify homes affected by sickness and death.

Harvesting

The small "berries" (actually fleshy cones) take three years to ripen completely. They can be picked and used fresh or dried once they turn dark blue.

Although they are suitable for flavouring, juniper berries are poisonous if eaten in large quantities.

Recommended

J. communis (common juniper) is the preferred species for juniper berry production. It is a small tree or shrub, and a large number of cultivars are available in a variety of sizes and forms.

Problems & Pests

Junipers are tough plants, but occasional problems may be caused by aphids, bagworms, bark beetles, canker, caterpillars, cedar-apple rust, leaf miners, mites, scale insects and twig blight.

J. communis var. *depressa*

J. communis var. *depressa*

The berries are used to flavour meat dishes and to give gin its distinctive flavour. They also make a nice addition to potpourri.

Kiwi

Actinidia

Features: woody, climbing, deciduous vine; early-summer flowers; edible fruit
Height: 4.5–9 m (15–30') **Spread:** indefinite **Hardiness:** zones 3–8

Hardy kiwi is handsome in its simplicity. Its lush green leaves, vigour and adaptability make it very useful, especially on difficult sites. The straight green of that species with blotches of pink and white added create the attractive variegated kiwi. Nursery catalogues make a convincing case for planting variegated kiwi—there is nothing else quite like it in the twining world. But it really doesn't perform like the pictures when it comes right out of the pot. A few years' maturity helps produce variegation, and very hot weather and shade will reduce it. Variegated kiwi does not grow as rampantly as hardy kiwi.

Growing

Kiwi vines grow best in **full sun**. The soil should be **fertile** and **well drained**. These plants require shelter from strong winds.

Prune in late winter. Plants can be trimmed to fit the area they've been given, or, if greater fruit production is desired, side shoots can be cut back to two or three buds from the main stems.

Tips

These vines need a sturdy structure to twine around. Pergolas, arbours and sufficiently large and sturdy fences provide good support. Given a trellis against a wall, a tree or some other upright structure, kiwis will twine upward all summer. They can also be grown in containers.

Kiwi vines can grow uncontrollably. Don't be afraid to prune them back if they are getting out of hand.

Harvesting

The fruit can be picked in late summer or autumn.

Recommended

A. arguta (hardy kiwi, bower actinidia) grows 6–9 m (20–30') tall but can be trained to grow lower through the judicious use of pruning shears. The leaves are dark green and heart shaped. White flowers are followed by smooth-skinned, greenish yellow, edible fruit.

A. kolomikta (variegated kiwi vine, kolomikta actinidia) grows 4.5–6 m (15–20') tall. The green leaves are strongly variegated with pink and white, and some of the leaves may be entirely white. White flowers are followed by smooth-skinned, greenish yellow, edible fruit. (Zones 4–8)

Problems & Pests

Kiwis are occasionally afflicted with fungal diseases, but these are not a serious concern.

The fruits of A. arguta *and* A. kolomikta *are hairless and high in vitamin C, potassium and fibre. These species make good substitutes for* A. chinensis *(*A. deliciosa*), the commercially available brown, hairy-skinned kiwi.*

A. arguta

Melon
Cucumis

Features: trailing vine; attractive foliage; yellow flowers **Height:** 30 cm (12")
Spread: 1.5–3 m (5–10') **Hardiness:** annual

Success with melons is somewhat limited in most Canadian gardens; they prefer warmer summer weather and a longer growing season than we can provide them. They are worth trying, though, and in the right spot, they can do really well. As an added bonus, they don't need as much water once the fruits are nearing their mature size, which is about the same time in late summer that it's easy to slack off on watering.

Growing

Melons grow best in **full sun** in a warm location. The soil should be **average to fertile, humus rich, moist** and **well drained**. Fruit develops poorly with inconsistent moisture, and plants can rot in cool or soggy soil. Use raised beds or mound the soil up before planting to improve drainage. The fruit will be sweeter and more flavourful if you cut back on watering as it is ripening.

Melons can be started indoors about six weeks before you want to transplant them to the garden. They don't like to have their roots disturbed, so plant them in fairly large peat pots so they have plenty of room to grow and can be set directly into the garden once the weather warms up. If you aren't sure how well melons will grow in your garden, try the short-season selections and plant them in the warmest part of the garden.

Tips

Melons have a well-deserved reputation for spreading, but like most vine-forming plants, they can be trained to grow up rather than out. As the fruit becomes larger, you may need to support it so the vines don't get damaged. You can create hammocks out of old nylon pantyhose to support the melons.

Melons have quite attractive foliage and can also be left to wind through your ornamental beds and borders.

Harvesting

Melons should be allowed to fully mature on the vine. Muskmelons develop more netting on the rind as they ripen. They generally slip easily from the vine with gentle pressure when ripe. Honeydew melons develop a paler colour when they are ripe. They must be cut from the vine when they are ripe.

Recommended

C. melo subsp. *reticulatus* (musk-melon) and *C. melo* subsp. *indorus* (honeydew melon) are tender annual vines with attractive green leaves. Bright yellow flowers are produced in summer. Male and female flowers are produced separately on the same vine. The melons are round, green or gold in colour and some, usually muskmelons, develop a corky tan or greenish netting as they ripen. Muskmelons generally develop orange or salmon-coloured flesh, and honeydew melons develop pale green or yellow flesh. Most melons take 70–85 days to produce mature, ripe fruit. Popular cultivars include **'Alaska,' 'Earlidew,' 'Earli-sweet,' 'Fastbreak,' 'Gourmet'** and **'Passport.'**

Problems & Pests

Powdery mildew, *Fusarium* wilt, cucumber beetles and sap beetles can be quite serious problems. Mildew weakens the plants, and the beetles may introduce wilt, which is fatal to the plants.

When maturity dates are given for fruits and vegetables, they usually refer to optimum conditions. Cool weather can greatly delay the development of your melons. Choose short-season varieties, and anticipate that you may need a longer season than suggested.

Mulberry
Morus

Features: slow-growing, long-lived shrub to medium tree; heart-shaped leaves; edible berries **Height:** 6–9 m (20–30') **Spread:** 6–9 m (20–30') **Hardiness:** zones 5–8

The mulberry, perhaps best known as a bush from the old nursery rhyme, also includes varieties that mature into large shade trees. Mulberry has attractive leaves and bark, and as the tree ages, branches develop interesting crooks and bends.

Growing
Mulberries are slow-growing and can take up to 10 years to mature. They fruit best in **full sun** and require **fertile, moist** soil.

They can be trained as large shrubs with many stems or as trees with a single trunk. Inspect older trees for brittle wood and, if need be, call in a professional to remove heavy, dangerous overhead branches.

Tips
Remember to site plants in a sunny spot well away from sidewalks, driveways and entrances. Falling fruit will stain concrete and is easily tracked into the house.

Harvesting
Pick fruit in late summer when fully ripe, though if you can't wait, slightly under-ripe fruit is good for cooking.

Recommended

M. alba (white mulberry) has red or pinkish white berries that are considered somewhat inferior for eating. However, it is the food of choice for silkworms. It was brought over from Asia a century ago and has since naturally hybridized with *M. rubra* and grows wild in many areas. **'Lavender'** bears lavender-white fruit and is said to be quite sweet. **'Whitey'** is a new grafted cultivar.

M. **'Illinois Everbearing'** is believed to be a hybrid of red and white mulberry and produces a flavourful berry.

M. nigra (black mulberry) has the attractive leaves and bark common to all mulberries, as well as near-black berries with a sharp, sweet flavour. **'Black Persian'** is a good variety to grow on the West Coast. **'Chelsea'** fruits early with dark red berries. **'Shah'** and **'Bachuus Noir'** are new grafted cultivars. **'Wellington'** is a heavy berry producer.

M. rubra (red mulberry) is native to the United States. It has red to black fruits and good autumn colour with bright yellow, heart-shaped leaves. **'Downing'** is a popular variety. New grafted cultivars to try are **'Pakistan'** and **'Red Gelato.'**

Problems & Pests

Birds are one of the few pests that trouble mulberries.

Folklore claims a fruiting mulberry is so attractive to birds that it will distract them from damaging other fruits.

M.alba (above), *M.alba* cultivar (below)

Olive

Olea

Features: gnarled tree; attractive bark; underside of the long, thin leaves is silvery **Height:** 7.5 m (25') **Spread:** 7.5–10 m (25–35') **Hardiness:** zones 9–10

*H*ardy, subtropical evergreens, olives require heat and warm, lengthy summers. The long-lived trees can endure some cold, but the fruit is damaged by the slightest frost.

Growing

Olives need **full sun** in a **sheltered** site protected from the wind. The soil should be **well drained**. They can be grown in containers but are unlikely to fruit. Home gardeners in the Pacific Northwest have varying degrees of luck overwintering olives outdoors. One daring grower on Pender Island off British Columbia's west coast is attempting Canada's first commercial olive grove.

Prune lightly. Fruit, if you're fortunate enough to have it set, grows on the previous season's wood.

Tips

The vast nightshade family includes poisonous plants such as belladonna as well as many popular vegetable garden plants. Avoid planting olives where tomatoes, potatoes, peppers, eggplants or tomatillos were previously grown.

Harvesting

In the Mediterranean, olive trees usually begin bearing fruit in their eighth year. When the fruit is firm and black, gather gently by hand to prevent bruising.

Olive trees are prized for oil as well as nutritious fruits that are too bitter to be eaten fresh. The fruits are treated with lye and then pickled or preserved in oil.

Recommended

O. europaea (common olive) is a beautiful tree with gnarled trunk, rough, grey bark and long, elegant leaves with silvery undersides. The flowers are white and fragrant. The grape-sized fruits are green, brown or black (and occasionally ivory). **'Arbequina'** is a variety often mentioned by home garden enthusiasts.

The Pender Island grower is trying the Italian varieties **'Frantoio'** and **'Leccino.'**

Problems & Pests

Possible problems with olives include *Verticillium* wilt and deer.

The quintessential emblem of the Mediterranean, the olive is an elegant and exceptionally long-lived tree.

Oregon Grapeholly
Mahonia

Features: upright, suckering, evergreen shrub; spring flowers; autumn fruit; late-autumn and winter foliage **Height:** 60 cm–2 m (2–7') **Spread:** 60 cm–2 m (2–7')
Hardiness: zones 5–9

Oregon grapeholly's name describes it well: it produces lustrous leaves similar to those of holly; the yellow, spring flowers are very showy; and the grape-like fruit contrasts beautifully with the glossy foliage. This broad-leafed, evergreen shrub benefits from careful placement and annual maintenance.

Growing

Oregon grapeholly prefers **light shade** or **partial shade** but tolerates full sun if the soil is moist. The soil should be of **average fertility, humus rich, moist** and **well drained**. Provide shelter from winter winds to prevent the foliage from drying out; exposed, windy sites will cause the leaves to become brown, dry and crunchy.

Awkward shoots can be removed in early summer. The growth can be irregular with a tendency to sucker, so an annual, artful pruning will lend Oregon grapeholly a more pleasing shape. Deadheading will keep the plant looking neat but will prevent the attractive, edible (though sour) fruit from forming.

Tips

Use this plant in shrub or mixed borders and in woodland gardens. Low-growing specimens can be used as groundcovers.

Harvesting

The dusky berries are ready to pick when they're plump and full, usually in early to mid-autumn.

Recommended

M. aquifolium grows 1–2 m (3–7') tall, with an equal spread. Bright yellow flowers appear in spring and are followed by clusters of purple or blue berries. The foliage turns

bronze-purple in late autumn and winter. **'Compactum'** is a low, mounding shrub with bronze foliage. It grows 60–90 cm (24–36") tall, with an equal spread.

Problems & Pests

Rust, leaf spot, gall and scale insects may cause occasional problems. Plants in exposed locations may develop leaf scorch in winter.

The juicy berries are edible, but very tart. They can be eaten fresh or used to make jellies, juices or wines.

Passionfruit
Passiflora

Features: exotic, purple-white flowers; attractive foliage **Height:** 1.5–3 m (5–10')
Spread: variable **Hardiness:** zones 6–9; often grown as an annual

*E*xotic and mesmerizing with fragrance and beauty, passionflower is sure to attract attention to your garden.

Growing
Passionflower grows well in **full sun** or **partial shade** in a location **sheltered** from wind and cold. The soil should be of **average fertility, moist** and **well drained**. A few selections are hardy to zone 6, and these vines may survive winter in some Canadian gardens.

Tips
Passionflower is a popular addition to mixed containers and creates an unusual focal point near a door or other entryway. Provided with a trellis or other structure, it will climb quickly all summer, though not as much as some of the other annual vines.

Harvesting
If you should ever be so lucky as to have fruit, leave it on the vine until it is fully ripe because it will not ripen further once picked. When fully ripe, the fruit will drop with a slight touch. Any leftover fruit pulp can be frozen with a little sugar and used to jazz up a fruit salad or dessert.

Recommended

P. caerulea (common passionflower, blue passionflower) is a vigorous, woody climber with deeply lobed leaves. It bears unusual purple-banded, purple-white flowers all summer. It can grow up to 9 m (30') tall, but usually grows only 1.5–3 m (5–10') tall over the course of a summer.

P. incarnata (maypop, purple passionflower) is a lovely climber that clings to the climbing surface with tendrils. It bears pale purple or white flowers with purple and white coronas all summer. This plant is hardy to zone 6. The vine dies back after frost, but the roots remain alive and send up foliage in spring around May.

Problems & Pests

Watch for aphids, spider mites and whiteflies.

In Bermuda, passionflower is made into perfume. Some people consider it an herb, and capsules said to aid sleep are found in health food stores.

Peach • Nectarine

Prunus

Features: rounded, small, deciduous tree; elegant, narrow leaves, pink, spring flowers; edible fruit **Height:** 1.8–4.5 m (6–15') **Spread:** 1.8–6 m (6–20')
Hardiness: zones 6–8

*P*eaches and nectarines are grown commercially in the Niagara peninsula of Ontario and coastal and southern interior areas of British Columbia. Over the years, they've undergone considerable tinkering to make them hardier, but the number of successful growing areas are smaller for these sublime fruits than for apples, plums or even cherries. Still, home gardeners blessed with a relatively benign climate may want to try their hand at growing peaches and/or nectarines.

Growing

Pick the growing site with care. Peaches and nectarines bloom early and require an area in the garden that warms early in spring and is protected from frost. **Full sun** and **deep, somewhat fertile, well-drained** soil are also essential.

Train trees to an open vase shape and prune every year, keeping the tree open to sunlight and low enough to pick the fruit easily. Thin the fruitlets gradually until the remaining fruitlets are a good hand-width apart.

Tips

Choose cultivars that are hardy, late-blooming and self-pollinating. Dwarf selections can be grown in containers. Peaches and nectarines can also be grown as espalier to conserve space.

Harvesting

The desire to grow peaches and nectarines is often stimulated by the dream of harvesting the fruit at the moment of perfection. Picked green, peaches and nectarines never have the juicy, aromatic, ambrosial quality of tree-ripened fruit. Ripe fruit will be soft around the stem and, because it bruises easily, should be picked with care. Rather than squeezing fruit to test for ripeness, it's better to visually check the area around the stem. That area is the last to ripen, and when the green colouration is almost gone, the fruit is ready to pick. Also, some growers say that when the fruit comes off the tree with no more than a gentle twist, it's ripe. Store with care, in single layers in boxes or on trays.

Recommended

P. persica includes peaches and nectarines. Nectarines are simply smooth-skinned peaches. The skins of peaches and nectarines vary in colour from yellow to orange-red, often with an attractive blush of red. Nectarine skin tends to be more deeply hued, often darkening to almost persimmon orange. The flesh

of peaches is yellow, sometimes with hints of red. There are also white-fleshed varieties of peaches. The flesh of nectarines varies from gold to deep amber and is firmer, more like a plum, and has a richer, subtle spicy flavour compared to that of peaches.

Freestone peaches are appreciated for out-of-hand eating and home canning. Cultivars include '**Elberta,**' an early-ripening variety; '**Glo Haven,**' a larger peach popular with home canners because it retains its flavour when cooked; and '**Red Haven,**' which is flavourful, leaf curl resistant and crops well. '**Stark Early White Giant**' is a disease-resistant variety of white-fleshed peach.

The flesh of clingstone peaches is more difficult to remove. Clingstones tend to have firmer, sturdier flesh, making them more suited to commercial canning. **'Mikado,'** a productive clingstone variety, needs cross-pollination.

Nectarine cultivars include **'Red Gold,'** a vigorous tree reaching 4.5 m (15') tall, and **'Sunglo,'** introduced from California in the early 1960s and often grown commercially.

Problems & Pests

Canker, leaf curl, powdery mildew, plum curculio weevils and tree borers are potential problems. Birds, aphids and red spider mites can also be troubling.

Botanists regard peach and nectarine as the same tree, pointing to the fact that a peach tree can grow from a nectarine pit, and vice versa. As well, peach trees sometimes produce fuzz-less peaches, and nectarines occasionally have fuzzy skin.

Peanut

Arachis

Features: bushy, potato-like habit; yellow flowers **Height:** 45 cm (18") **Spread:** 30 cm (12") **Hardiness:** annual

*P*eanuts are highly nutritious and self-pollinating. They can endure light frost and, with a long, warm growing season, produce an edible crop. On a commercial basis, peanuts have been grown in southern Ontario since the 1980s.

Growing

Grow peanuts in **full sun**. The soil should be **light, well worked** and preferably **sandy**. With the ability to "fix" their own nitrogen, they require little additional fertilization.

Plant in mid-spring in hills, 4 kernels to a mound, no deeper than 5 cm (2") to encourage quicker growth. Peanuts can be planted in the shell or hulled. They require lots of sunshine and warmth, and if the days are cool and cloudy at planting time, germination will be slow.

When plants reach about 30 cm (12") in height, hill as you would potatoes. After hilling, a good mulch of straw or grass clippings is beneficial. Keep hills 60 cm (24") apart. After pollination, shoots form at the base of the flower and push down into the soil, eventually maturing into pods. Each plant will produce 20 to 25 pods or peanuts.

Tips

Start peanuts indoors, about a month before the last spring frost usually occurs, to provide the longest possible growing season.

Harvesting

Harvest in late autumn, but before the threat of serious frost, when the plant's leaves begin to yellow. Gently lift the bush out of the ground and shake it to loosen and remove soil. Store peanuts in a shallow layer in a warm, dry place for at least two months before roasting. They can also made into a spread or cooking oil.

Recommended

A. hypogaea grows underground from a yellow-flowered, potato-like plant whose stalks have pushed down into the soil and produced pods. These pods have thin, light brown, easily-shelled husks that contain a small number of red-skinned, beige seeds (peanuts). It comes in four basic types: runner, Virginia, Spanish and Valencia. Canadian growers will likely have the best luck with a runner (try **'Florunner'**) or Valencia type.

Problems & Pests

With hilling and good mulch, peanuts suffer few problems.

Although often thought of as a nut, the peanut is actually a member of the pea, or legume, family.

Pear

Pyrus

Features: conical, rounded or pyramidal, deciduous tree; spring flowers; summer and autumn foliage; fruit **Height:** 4.5–15 m (15–50') **Spread:** 3.6–15 m (12–50')
Hardiness: zones 4–8

When the full moon and full flowering of the Callery pear cultivars coincide in spring on a cloudless night, the trees look like an earthly Milky Way. Even under less spectacular circumstances, their show of white is something to behold. Unfortunately, the many 'Bradford' cultivars have broken many a gardener's heart, but even though other types are not as formal in shape or quite as burgundy in autumn, there are several good alternatives to choose from. Whether you are looking for an individual specimen or wish to line your driveway or street with nicely uniform trees, other pears can do the job. Just look for, and prune to create, good branch spacing and wide crotch angles.

Growing

Pears grow best in **full sun**. The soil should preferably be **fertile** and **well drained**, but pears adapt to most well-drained soils.

Remove dead or damaged growth as needed, and do what little formative pruning is required in winter or early spring.

Tips

Pears, like apples, are popular for use as espalier specimens. Their reasonable size and pollution tolerance makes them good specimen trees for medium and some smaller city gardens.

Harvesting

Unlike many fruits, pears must be picked early and not allowed to ripen on the tree. If left on the tree, they develop hard, gritty cells and the flesh begins to rot. The best time to harvest is when the fruit is well-shaped and comes easily from the tree yet is still too firm to eat. Pick carefully; the thin skin can be easily bruised or pierced. Store pears in a cool place and eat or cook as they ripen. To slow ripening, keep pears in the refrigerator.

P. calleryana CHANTICLEER (above)

Recommended

P. calleryana (Callery pear) is a conical tree with thorny branches. It grows 9–15 m (30–50') tall with an equal spread. It is covered in clusters of white flowers in mid-spring. Small, brown fruits ripen in autumn as the glossy, green foliage turns red. The species is rarely grown, but many attractive cultivars have been developed. ARISTOCRAT ('Aristocrat') is a pyramidal tree that maintains a strong central leader. Leaves turn shades of yellow through red in autumn. **'Bradford'** is an older cultivar that is **no longer recommended** because the narrow branch angles cause the many branches on older trees to break off, with entire trees sometimes splitting down the mid-

dle. BURGUNDY SNOW ('Burgozam') bears white flowers that have burgundy centres. CHANTICLEER ('Cleveland Select,' 'Select,' 'Stone Hill') is a narrow, pyramidal, thornless cultivar that grows about 12 m (40') tall and spreads about 6 m (20'). It is resistant to fire blight. CLEVELAND PRIDE ('Cleprizam') has a pyramidal habit. The new foliage emerges pink. GLADIATOR ('Gladzam') is a vigorous grower with a pyramidal habit. REDSPIRE ('Redspire') is a thornless, pyramidal cultivar. The leaves turn yellow in autumn. TRINITY ('Trinity') is a round cultivar that grows about 9 m (30') tall, with an equal spread. It flowers profusely, and its leaves turn scarlet in autumn. VALIANT ('Valzam') has a columnar to pyramidal habit. It grows 9 m (30') tall and spreads 6 m (20'). With the continued selection and testing that is currently underway, there should be some interesting new dwarf cultivars available in the near future. (Zones 5–8)

P. salicifolia (willow-leaved pear) is a rounded, spreading tree that grows 4.5–7.5 m (15–25') tall with an equal spread. It has narrow, willow-like, fuzzy, grey leaves. It bears clusters of white flowers in spring and green, pear-shaped fruit in autumn. SILVERFROST ('Silfrozam') is an attractive, broadly weeping cultivar. It grows about 4.5 m (15') tall and spreads about 3.6 m (12'). (Zones 4–7)

Problems & Pests

Fire blight is fairly common and can be a big problem, though it tends to be the worst on common pear (*P. communis*). Caterpillars, scale insects, anthracnose, canker and powdery mildew can also cause trouble.

Pears are one of the most attractive flowering trees, especially when covered in clouds of white flowers in spring.

Pecan • Hickory
Carya

Features: medium to large tree; large leaves turn gold in autumn; clustered husked nuts **Height:** 15–30 m (50–100') **Spread:** 7.5–9 m (25–30') **Hardiness:** zones 5–9

*H*ickories and pecans are closely related and have been hybridized to create "hicans" in the hope of combining the most desirable characteristics of each nut into one nut.

Growing
Plant in **full sun** at least 10 m (33') apart to allow for a massive root system in **deep, fertile, well-drained** soil. Don't plant too deep; aim for the depth at which it was grown in the nursery. Because they're self-fertile, only a single pecan or hican is required to produce nuts.

Tips
Take into account the large space a mature tree will occupy and avoid planting under power lines or too close to buildings. Also plant well away from sidewalks, lawns and rooftops where falling nuts will create problems.

Harvesting
Pick the nuts when they begin to fall. If you don't want to hand-pick, try the limb-shaking method, being careful not to damage the branches. Spread nuts in a single layer in a warm, sheltered area such as an attic

C. illinoinensis

or garage to dry, turning them occasionally, then store them in a cool spot.

Recommended

C. illinoinensis (pecan) is a large tree with elongated, somewhat glossy leaves and insignificant flowers. The nut resembles a walnut, though the pecan's reddish shell is smooth. **'Cheyenne'** is a smaller but productive tree with choice nuts. **'Mohawk'** is thin-shelled and produces large pecans that crack easily into the perfect halves that are desirable for baking. **'Stuart'** is an improved hardy variety of pecan.

C. laciniosa (shellbark hickory) and *C. ovata* (shagbark hickory) have striking peeling bark and attractive golden leaves in autumn. Hickories grow in the wild and produce edible but hard-shelled, small nuts. Breeders in the United States have developed the shellbarks **'Keystone'** and **'Missouri Mammoth'** to produce choice, cleanly-cracking nuts. Good shagbarks for tasty, thin-shelled nuts are **'Wilcox'** and **'Yoder.'**

Crosses between *C. illinoinensis* and *C. ovata* have resulted in hybrids called hicans. Good varieties suited to our northern gardens are **'Burton,' 'Fairbanks,' 'Hales'** and **'Henke.'**

Problems & Pests

These trees are relatively problem-free with good maintenance practices.

Pecans tolerate frost but need a long, hot summer to produce edible nuts.

C. illinoinensis

Persimmon

Diospyros

Features: medium, deciduous tree; glossy leaves; cream flowers; sweet, autumn fruit **Height:** 6–9 m (20–30') **Spread:** 5–9 m (16–30') **Hardiness:** zones 5–8

*P*ersimmons, tasting of honey and plums, are an especially elegant fruit with gleaming orange skin and a graceful rounded or heart-shaped form.

Growing

Persimmon trees prefer **full sun** in a **sheltered** location because the wood is fairly brittle and easily damaged. Plant the trees 2.5 cm (1") deeper than they grew in the nursery, in **well-drained** soil. Allow a 5–6 m (16–20') space for each plant, and take care not to damage the long, delicate taproot.

Persimmons require little more maintenance than light pruning to remove broken branches and chopping back the numerous suckers. It's also a good idea, if the fruit is very heavy, to do some hand-thinning to lighten the load on the branches.

Tips

As a general rule, Oriental persimmon does not need pollination to set fruit, but most American persimmon varieties do. For best crops, grow plants of both sexes.

Harvesting

Let American and the astringent-type Oriental persimmons ripen until they're well-coloured and very soft. Varieties of Oriental persimmons that are eaten firm should be harvested as soon as they are fully coloured. Persimmons that must be picked underripe can be ripened indoors with varying degrees of success.

Recommended

D. kaki (Oriental persimmon) fruit looks like a tomato and, depending on the variety, can have either a crisp or jelly-like texture. The large **'Fuyu'** is often the one you'll find in the supermarket and is usually eaten while still firm. **'Hachiya'** is more cone-shaped and should be enjoyed when it's soft.

D. virginiana (American persimmon) fruit is smaller with richer, drier flesh than its Asian cousin. **'Meader'** and **'Pieper'** are better adapted to cooler regions.

D. kaki 'Hachiya'

Problems & Pests

Persimmons are pretty much pest-free.

Meaning "food for the gods," Diospyros *is an apt description of this delectable, strikingly handsome fruit.*

D. kaki 'Fuyu'

Pine Nut
Pinus

Features: upright, columnar or spreading, evergreen tree; foliage; bark; cones
Height: 60 cm–35 m (2–115') **Spread:** 60 cm–15 m (2–50') **Hardiness:** zones 2–8

P. mugo

*P*ines are more diverse and widely adapted than any other conifer. From the towering, picturesque Michigan native white pine to the shrubby, low, mounded mugo pine, this vast genus offers a wide array of interesting landscape plants. Pines are usually grown for landscaping purposes, but they do produce an edible seed or "nut." Most pines' seeds are edible, though many are too small to bother with. Commercially available pine nuts come from *P. pinea* and other species. There is at least one pine nut tree nursery in southern Ontario.

Growing

Pines grow best in **full sun**. They adapt to most **well-drained** soils. These trees are not heavy feeders. Fertilizing will encourage rapid new growth that is weak and susceptible to pest and disease problems.

Generally, little or no pruning is required. Hedges can be trimmed in midsummer. Pinch up to one-half the length of the "candles," the fully extended but still soft new growth, to shape the plant or to regulate growth.

Tips

Pines can be used as specimen trees, hedges or windbreaks. Large pines can be used to create rich green backdrops for your smaller ornamentals. Smaller species and cultivars can be mixed into a border to provide texture and interest year-round.

Harvesting

To harvest the nuts, collect the cones, spread them on plastic sheeting or concrete and let them dry until they open up. The nuts that fall out need to be shelled and then, because of their high oil content, kept refrigerated to prevent rancidity.

Recommended

P. aristata (bristlecone pine) is a fairly small, slow-growing pine with a conical or shrubby habit. It grows 2.4–9 m (8–30') tall and spreads 1.8–6 m (6–20'). It does not tolerate pollution but survives in poor, dry, rocky soil. Needles may dry out in windy winter locations. (Zones 4–8)

P. cembra (Swiss stone pine) has a dense, columnar habit. It grows 9–21 m (30–70') tall and spreads 4.5–7.5 m (15–25'). This slow-growing pine is resistant to white pine blister rust. (Zones 3–7)

"Methuselah," a bristlecone pine that grows high in the White Mountains of California, is more than 4700 years old—the world's oldest known living thing.

P. mugo

P. mugo (mugo pine) is a low, rounded, spreading shrub or tree. It grows 3–6 m (10–20') tall and spreads 4.5–6 m (15–20'). **Var. *pumilio*** (var. *pumilo*) is a dense variety that forms a mound 60 cm–2.4 m (2–8') tall and wide. Its slow growth and small size make it a good choice for planters and rock gardens. (Zones 2–7)

P. parviflora (Japanese white pine) grows 6–21 m (20–70') tall and spreads 6–15 m (20–50'). It is conical or columnar when young and matures to a spreading crown. This species has been used to create bonsai. (Zones 4–8)

P. strobus (eastern white pine) is a slender, conical tree that grows 15–35 m (50–115') tall and spreads 6–12 m (20–40'). It has soft, plumy needles and is sometimes grown as a hedge. Young trees can be killed by white pine blister rust, but mature

P. cembra (left), *P. sylvestris* (below)

specimens are resistant. **'Fastigiata'** is an attractive narrow, columnar form that grows up to 21 m (70') tall. **'Nana'** is a dwarf cultivar that grows about 90 cm (36") tall and spreads up to 1.8 m (6'). **'Pendula'** has long, ground-sweeping branches. It must be trained to form an upright leader when young to give it some height and shape; otherwise, it can be grown as a groundcover or left to spill over the top of a rock wall or slope. It develops an unusual soft, shaggy, droopy appearance as it matures. (Zones 3–8)

P. sylvestris (Scots pine, Scotch pine) grows 9–21 m (30–70') tall and spreads 6–12 m (20–40'). It is rounded or conical when young and develops an irregular, flat-topped, spreading habit when mature. Trees of this species vary in size, habit, needle colour and needle length. Young Scots pines are popular as Christmas trees. (Zones 2–7)

Problems & Pests

Blight, blister rust, borers, caterpillars, cone rust, leaf miners, mealybugs, pitch canker, sawflies, scale insects and tar spot can all cause problems. The European pine-shoot moth attacks pines with needles in clusters of two or three.

There's an easy way to distinguish pines from other needled evergreens. Pine needles are grouped together in bundles, while spruce, fir and hemlock needles are borne singly.

Austrian pine (P. nigra) was long recommended as the pine most tolerant of urban conditions. Unfortunately, overplanting has led to severe disease problems, some of which can lead to a tree's death within a single growing season.

Pineapple
Ananas

Features: tropical plant with dagger-like leaves; flower stock has light blue blossoms that bloom for a single day **Height:** 90 cm–1.2 m (3–4') **Spread:** 1.5–1.8 m (5–6')
Hardiness: tropical perennial grown as a greenhouse specimen or houseplant

Pineapple is a short-lived perennial much too tender for our Canadian climate, but it can be grown as a novel houseplant or in a greenhouse.

Growing

To grow as a houseplant, cut the stem from a purchased pineapple, maintaining a bit of attached flesh. Scrape off the flesh and put the stem cutting in a small bowl of water until a root forms. Transplant to a container with **well-drained** potting soil and plenty of **compost**. Feed every 8 to 12 weeks with a liquid fertilizer, moderately high in potassium and high in nitrogen. In the greenhouse, plant rooted cuttings or "slips" in pots of compost and apply a liquid feed every three weeks.

Water diligently and use an organic mulch to conserve moisture. At flowering time, use a support stake to protect the young fruit.

Tips

Place your pineapple container in the brightest, sunniest area in your home.

Harvesting

Harvest fruits when they turn yellow and develop a sweet aroma, about 20 months after the slips are potted up. Cut the stem 2.5 cm (1") below each fruit.

Recommended

A. comosus resembles yucca, a common plant in xeriscape gardens. It has handsome, sometimes spiny, blade-shaped, green and gold leaves and a red bud cluster of approximately 150 flowers. These flowers, arranged in a spiral pattern, open when the cluster reaches a length of 5–7.5 cm (2–3"). Each of the pale blue flowers blooms for a single day. Many older varieties of pineapple have disappeared due to the few commercial cultivars that now dominate the industry, but **'Smooth Cayenne'** is still available. It has no spines on its leaves and makes a good container plant.

Problems & Pests

Potential problems are heart rot, mites and mealybugs.

Pineapple, now synonymous with Hawaii, hails from northern South America and is considered a symbol of hospitality.

Plum

Prunus

Features: upright, rounded, spreading or weeping, deciduous tree or shrub; spring to early-summer flowers; fruit; bark; autumn foliage **Height:** 1–9 m (3–30') **Spread:** 1–9 m (3–30') **Hardiness:** zones 3–9

*P*lums are extremely varied fruits. Their colours run the gamut from yellow and green to red and purple. They can be as small as a grape or as large as a peach. And their taste ranges from mouth-puckering tangy to sublimely sweet. Plums also lend themselves to hybridization with other stone fruit, which has resulted in successful crosses such as the delightfully named pluot.

Growing

These flowering fruit trees prefer **full sun**. The soil should be of **average fertility, moist** and **well drained**. Plant on mounds when possible to encourage drainage. Shallow roots will emerge from the ground if the tree is not getting sufficient water.

Some plums are self-fertile, but for good fruit production, all plums benefit from another tree of the same family nearby. For success in colder areas, down to zone 3, choose dwarf stock grafted with hardy root-stock.

After flowering is finished, remove damaged growth and awkward branches as required. Plums grown as shrubs or trees need very little pruning. Hedges can be trimmed back after flowering is complete.

Tips

Plums are beautiful as specimen plants, and many are small enough to be included in almost any garden. Purpleleaf dwarf plum can be trained to form a small tree in space-restricted gardens. Small species and cultivars can also be included in borders or grouped to form hedges or barriers.

Harvesting

A mature plum tree can easily deliver 10–25 kg (20–55 lb) of fruit. In late summer or early autumn, the ripened, richly coloured fruits of Italian prune trees have a hazy, powdery "bloom" and are easily plucked from the tree. Other varieties may ripen sooner, so if they're plump and leave the tree readily, they're ready for harvest. Plums freeze well and are easily dried in an electric fruit dryer.

Recommended

P. americana hybrids, which are crosses with wild native American plums and other species, often hardy Japanese varieties, are some of the best plums for Canada's colder regions. 'Percy's' is vigorous and productive. The fruits are small, 4 cm (1½") in diameter, with sweet, juicy, yellow flesh. (Zones 3–9)

P. salicina cultivar (below)

***P. cerasifera* 'Atropurpurea'** (Pissard plum) is a shrubby, often multi-stemmed tree that grows 6–9 m (20–30') tall, with an equal spread. Light pink flowers that fade to white emerge before the deep purple foliage. The leaves turn dark green as they mature. **'Newport'** was bred by crossing 'Atropurpurea' back to the species (*P. cerasifera*). The new cultivar is more cold hardy and flowers earlier. (Zones 4–8)

P.* x *cistena (purpleleaf dwarf plum, purpleleaf sand cherry) is a dainty, upright shrub that grows 1.5–3 m (5–10') tall, with an equal or lesser spread. The deep purple leaves keep their colour all season. The fragrant, white or slightly pink flowers open in mid- to late spring after the leaves have developed. The fruit ripens to purple-black in July. (Zones 3–8)

P. domestica 'Italian Prune' grows 4.5–6 m (15–20') tall with an equal spread. The leaves are crisp and moderately veined, and the rough bark varies from grey to brown. White flowers produce large, purple-black fruits with gold flesh that ripen in late summer or early autumn and are excellent for eating fresh or drying. (Zones 5–9)

P. institia (Damson plum) is a heavy bearing, small-leaved, shrubby tree, up to 3 m (10') tall with a similar spread, and can often be found still growing on abandoned farms and old orchard land. The small, dark purple fruits are best used for cooking and are often made into preserves or jams. (Zones 5–9)

P. x cistena (above)

P. domestica cultivar (below)

P. pluot is a 75% plum, 25% apricot hybrid that looks much like a plum with its round shape and shiny, smooth skin but has sweeter skin than that of a true plum. **'Flavor King Pluot,'** a registered variety, resembles a Santa Rosa plum and has reddish purple skin and attractive red flesh. It has a spicy bouquet and taste, produces especially attractive white flowers and reaches an overall height and spread of 4 m (13'). Other apricot-plum hybrids include the aprium (less plum, more apricot) and plumcot (a 50/50 cross). (Zones 6–9)

P. salicina 'Santa Rosa' grows 4–4.5 m (13–15') tall with an equal or lesser spread and has an upright habit with upward-growing branches. It blooms

early and bears a light crop of large, round, somewhat heart-shaped, reddish purple plums dusted with a blue bloom. The juicy, amber flesh is tinged with red and is delicious eaten fresh on its own or in salads. (Zones 6–9)

Problems & Pests

The many possible problems include aphids, borers, caterpillars, leafhoppers, mites, nematodes, plum curculio weevils, scale insects, canker, crown gall, fire blight, powdery mildew and viruses. Root rot can occur in poorly drained soils.

Pissard plum was one of the first purple-leaved cultivars, introduced into cultivation in 1880.

Prickly Pear
Opuntia

Features: evergreen cactus; thick, oval, fleshy, spine-covered pads; white, yellow or red flowers; egg-sized, pear-shaped fruit with skin ranging from yellow to lime green to magenta with yellowy green or reddish purple flesh **Height:** 90 cm–1.8 m (3–6') **Spread:** 3–4.5 m (10–15') **Hardiness:** zones 5–8

Prickly pear, also known as prickly pear cactus, hides a somewhat bland, seedy interior behind a barb-tufted, spiny outer skin and a thick second under-layer that must be removed with glove-protected hands before eating. Nevertheless, the fruit is enormously popular in many parts of the world including the Mediterranean, South Africa, Australia, Mexico and South America.

Growing

If trying prickly pears outdoors, grow them in **full sun** in a **sheltered** spot protected from both wind and rain. The soil should be **well drained** and **alkaline**.

Keep prickly pear well-weeded and, if needed, use a prop to support the pads.

Tips

Prickly pears need a long, warm growing season and in Canada are perhaps best grown in a large container to overwinter indoors or a greenhouse.

Harvesting
Both pads and fruit are edible. In its native habitat, prickly pear tolerates several harvests of its pads in a year. Once picked, the fruit will last a week or more and can be used in fruit cups or salads, or made into jam.

Recommended
O. engelmannii (Engelmann's prickly pear) grows 1.5 m (5') tall and has blue-green pads, showy yellow flowers and large, juicy fruit.

O. violacea var. *santa-rita* (purple prickly pear) grows 90 cm (3') tall and has blue-purple pads, yellow flowers and white or black spines. In winter or during drought conditions, the pads turn red or purple.

Problems & Pests
Prickly pear has relatively few problems.

O. polyacantha, *a low-growing species, is hardy as far north as North Dakota.*

Quince
Cydonia

Features: small, self-fertile, shrubby tree; attractive pink and white, apple-like blossoms; round or pear-shaped, aromatic fruit **Height:** 6–7.5 m (20–25') **Spread:** 3.6–4.5 m (12–15') **Hardiness:** zones 5–8

Quince is a beautiful ornamental tree that perfumes the garden with a wild, musky, tropical fragrance. Sadly, its popularity has declined over the years, perhaps because the sour, ivory-fleshed fruit must be cooked to be palatable. Quince shines in fruit desserts, savory main dishes and preserves and jellies.

Growing
Quince prefers **full sun**. A bright, **sheltered** site is best. The soil should be **deep, light** and **moist**. Plant two-year-old stock and fertilize sparingly. Maintain a good mulch of organic material. Prune straggly growth and crossing branches in late winter or early spring.

Tips
This moisture-lover grows best and looks lovely near a pond or stream. Quince can also be grown as a bush along a south-facing wall.

Harvesting
Be patient! It will often take upward of five years for the first crop, but then you can expect a good yield for the next 40 years. When ripe, fruit will release readily from the branch with no more than a slight tug.

Handle gently to avoid bruising the delicate skin, and store in a cool, dark place for up to two months. Keep separate from pears and apples, which tend to absorb quince's musky fragrance.

Recommended

C. oblonga has yellow, pear- or apple-shaped fruits covered with a downy skin. The green, apple-like leaves have a downy underside and turn a lovely golden yellow in autumn. **'Champion'** is cold hardy and ripens large, round fruit in early October. **'Vranja'** produces good-sized, pear-shaped fruit.

Problems & Pests

Possible pest and disease problems are similar to apple trees.

Quince fruits offer calcium and iron and quantities of natural pectin, making them ideal for preserves and fruit leather.

Raspberry • Blackberry

Rubus

Features: thicket-forming shrub; long, arching canes; spring flowers; summer fruit
Height: 1–3 m (3–10') **Spread:** 1.2–1.5 m (4–5') or more **Hardiness:** zones 3–8

The sweet, juicy berries of these shrubs are popular for use in pies, jams and other fruit desserts, but they are just as delicious when eaten fresh. Thickets are often pruned and staked to form neat rows but can be left to spread freely if you have the space.

Growing

Raspberries and blackberries grow well in **full sun, light shade** or **partial shade**, though the best fruiting occurs in full sun. The soil should be of **average fertility, humus rich, moist** and **well drained**. These plants prefer a location **sheltered** from strong winds. Blackberries, in particular, are prone to winter damage.

Bare-root canes should be purchased in late winter or early spring and should preferably be planted while they are still dormant. Container-grown plants are often available all season, though they may not establish as well.

Blackberries have very long, flexible canes, and though they can stand freely without staking, they may take up less room if they are kept tidy by being loosely tied to a supportive structure such as a stout post or fence. Prune out some of the older canes each year once plants become established to keep plants vigorous and to control the spread.

Tips

These shrubs form rather formidable thickets and can be used in shrub and mixed borders, along fences and as hedges.

Harvesting

Pick fruit as soon as it is ripe in mid- to late summer. The fruit does not all ripen at once, and you can harvest it for a month or more. Some raspberry varieties are ever-bearing and produce fruit in flushes from midsummer through autumn.

Many other Rubus *species grow well in Canada, including cloudberry, loganberry and wineberry.*

Recommended

R. fruticosus (blackberry, bramble) forms a thicket of thorny stems or canes. Canes can grow up to 3 m (10') long, and thickets can spread 1.5 m (5') or more. White, or occasionally pink, late-spring or early-summer flowers are followed by red or black berries in late summer. Thornless varieties are available. (Zones 5–8)

R. idaeus (raspberry) forms a thicket of bristly stems or canes. Canes grow 1–1.5 m (3–5') long, and thickets can spread 1.2 m (4') or more. White, spring flowers are followed by red, yellow, black or purple fruit in mid-summer. Raspberries fall into two categories: summer-bearing and ever-bearing. Although raspberry shrubs are perennial, the canes are biennial, generally growing the first

year and producing fruit the second. In the third season, the cane dies back. Ever-bearing canes begin to fruit late in the season of their first autumn, then again the second summer. They are suitable where autumn is long and warm; summer-bearing varieties are more suitable for short-season areas.

Problems & Pests

Problems with anthracnose, powdery mildew, rust, fire blight, leaf-hoppers and caterpillars can occur.

If you have more fruit than you can use fresh, spread the excess out on a paper-lined cookie sheet and freeze it. Transfer the fruit to a plastic bag once it is frozen.

Rhubarb

Rheum

Features: clump-forming perennial; red or green stems; large, deeply veined leaves; spikes of flowers in summer **Height:** 60 cm–1.2 m (2–4') **Spread:** 90 cm–1.8 m (3–6') **Hardiness:** zones 2–8

*L*ike tomatoes, rhubarb treads the fine line between fruit and vegetable. Although it is actually a vegetable, we usually eat it in fruit dishes and think of it more as a fruit.

Growing

Rhubarb grows best in **full sun**. The soil should be **fertile, humus rich, moist** and **well drained**, though this plant adapts to most conditions. A fertile soil encourages more and bigger stems. Gently work some compost into the soil around the rhubarb each year, and add a layer of compost mulch.

Rhubarb can be started from seed sown directly in the garden, or crowns can be purchased in spring. If you've planted crowns, you can begin harvesting the second summer, while seeded plants may take three or more years before they produce harvestable stems. If a friend or neighbour has a rhubarb plant, you can ask for a division from that plant.

Rhubarb can stay in one spot for many years, but it will be more vigorous and productive if divided every eight or so years. Work some more compost in when you divide

the plant. Roots can be broken into smaller sections; each piece will sprout as long as it has an "eye."

Tips
Sadly, this stunning plant is often relegated to back corners and waste areas in the garden. With its dramatic leaves, bright red stems and intriguing flowers, it deserves a far more central location.

Harvesting
Harvest the stems by pulling them firmly and cleanly from the base of the plant. The leaves can then be cut from the stems with a sharp knife and composted or spread around the base of the plant to conserve moisture, suppress weed growth and return nutrients to the soil. Don't remove more than half the stems from the plant in one year. Rhubarb's flavour is better earlier in summer, and harvesting generally stops by early July, when the stems start to become dry, pithy and bitter.

Recommended
R. rhabarbarum and **R. x hybridum** form large clumps of glossy, deeply veined, green, bronzy or reddish leaves. The edible stems can be green, red or a bit of both. Spikes of densely clustered red, yellow or green flowers are produced in midsummer. Popular varieties include **'Colossal,'** with huge leaves and stems, **'Crimson Cherry'** and **'Victoria.'**

Problems & Pests
Rhubarb rarely suffers from any problems.

Although the flowers are quite interesting and attractive, they are often removed to prolong the stem harvest.

Only the stems of rhubarb are edible. The leaves contain oxalic acid in toxic quantities.

Rosehip
Rosa

Features: dense, arching habit; clove-scented, mauve-purple or mauve-red, early-summer to autumn flowers; orange-red hips **Height:** 1.2–1.5 m (4–5') **Spread:** 1.5–1.8 m (5–6') **Hardiness:** zones 3–8

*H*ansa, first introduced in 1905, is one of the most durable, long-lived and versatile roses.

Growing

Hansa grows best in **full sun**. The soil should preferably be **average to fertile, humus rich, slightly acidic, moist** and **well drained**, but this durable rose adapts to most soils from silty clay to sand.

Remove a few of the oldest canes every few years to keep the plants blooming vigorously.

Tips

Rugosa roses such as Hansa make good additions to mixed borders and beds and can also be used as hedges or as specimens. They are often used on steep banks to prevent soil erosion, and the prickly branches keep people from walking through flower beds and compacting the soil.

Harvesting

Pick rosehips in late summer when they are firm, full and well-coloured. Avoid soft, over-ripe ones. For a herbal tea rich in vitamin C, trim

both blossom and stem ends, halve the hip and scrape out the seeds. Dry the halves on screens indoors until they're as hard as a coffee bean. Use a blender or old coffee mill to grind them up. Rosehips also make a beautiful pink-hued jelly, and rose petals can be candied to garnish desserts or salads or made into rose water.

Recommended

R. rugosa 'Hansa' is a bushy shrub with arching canes and leathery, deeply veined, bright green leaves. The double flowers are produced all summer. The bright orange hips persist into winter. Other rugosa roses include 'Blanc Double de Coubert,' with white, double flowers that are produced all summer.

Problems & Pests

Blackspot, rust, mildew, aphids, Japanese beetles, spider mites and slugs can attack roses.

Rosa rugosa is a wide-spreading plant with disease-resistant foliage—a trait it has passed on to the many hybrids and cultivars that are available.

Serviceberry
Saskatoon, Juneberry
Amelanchier

Features: single- or multi-stemmed, deciduous large shrub or tree; spring or early-summer flowers; edible fruit; autumn colour; bark **Height:** 2.1–9 m (7–30') **Spread:** 1.5–9 m (5–30') **Hardiness:** zones 3–9

The news continues to spread about the charms of serviceberry specimens. *Amelanchier* species are first-rate North American natives, and breeders have refined the habits to make them more useful in the home landscape. The small trees bear lacy, white flowers in spring, followed by edible berries. In autumn, the foliage colour ranges from a glowing apricot to deep red. Artistic branch growth showing in winter makes these excellent trees all year long.

Growing

Serviceberry grows well in **full sun** or **light shade**. The soil should be **fertile, acidic, humus rich, moist** and **well drained**, though serviceberry will tolerate alkaline soil and adjust to drought.

Very little pruning is needed. Young plants, particularly multi-stemmed ones, can be pruned to encourage healthy, attractive growth and form; only the strongest, healthiest stems should be allowed to remain. Dead,

damaged, diseased and awkward branches can be removed as needed.

Tips

Serviceberries make beautiful specimen plants or even shade trees in small gardens. The shrubby forms can be grown along the edge of a woodland or in a border and are especially attractive in a naturalized planting. In the wild, these trees are often found growing near water sources, and they make beautiful pond- or streamside plants.

A serviceberry bush underplanted with a groundcover and bulbs makes a richly textured spring composition.

Harvesting

The fruit ripens all at once in midsummer, facilitating one major picking. Be prepared for purple finger stains! The fruit can be used in the place of blueberries in any recipe, having a similar, but generally sweeter flavour.

A. canadensis (above)
A. x grandiflora (below)

Recommended

A. arborea (downy serviceberry, june-berry) forms a small, single- or multi-stemmed tree. It grows 4.5–7.5 m (15–25') tall and spreads 4.5–9 m (15–30'). Clusters of fragrant, white flowers are borne in spring. The edible berries ripen to reddish purple in summer. In autumn, the foliage turns to shades ranging from yellow to red. (Zones 4–9)

A. canadensis (shadblow service-berry) forms a large, upright, suck-ering shrub. It grows 2–6 m (7–20') tall and spreads 1.5–4.5 m (5–15'). White, spring flowers are followed by edible, dark purple fruit in sum-mer. The foliage turns orange and red in autumn. This species toler-ates moist, boggy soil conditions. (Zones 3–8)

A. x *grandiflora* (apple serviceberry) is a small, spreading, often multi-stemmed tree. It grows 6–9 m (20–30') tall, with an equal spread. New foliage is often bronze coloured, then turns green over summer and bright orange or red in autumn. White, spring flowers are followed by purple fruit in summer. In cold areas of Canada, plant this species in a sheltered spot to protect it during winter. **'Ballerina'** has bright red autumn colour and is fire blight resistant. (Zones 4–8)

Problems & Pests

Problems with rust, fire blight, powdery mildew, leaf miners, borers and leaf spot can occur but are generally not serious.

A. canadensis (all photos)

Birds are attracted to the garden by the ripening fruit and may eat all the berries before you get a chance to pick any.

Squash

Cucurbita

Features: trailing or mounding habit; large, lobed, decorative leaves; colourful flowers and fruit **Height:** 45–60 cm (18–24") **Spread:** 60 cm–3 m (2–10') **Hardiness:** annual

Squash are generally grouped as summer squash and winter squash. This reflects when we eat them more than any real difference in the plants themselves. All squash develop hardened rinds in autumn if left to mature. The squash that keep the longest and have the best taste and texture when mature are grouped as winter squash. Summer squash are tender and tasty when they are immature but tend to become stringy and sometimes bitter when they mature, and they don't keep as well.

Growing

Squash grow best in **full sun** but tolerate light shade from companion plants. The soil should be **fertile, humus rich, moist** and **well drained**. Squash generally need a long, warm summer to develop well. Gardeners in cooler areas will want to choose cultivars that mature in a shorter season.

Start seeds in peat pots indoors six to eight weeks early. Keep them in as bright a location as possible to reduce stretching. Plant out or direct sow after the last frost date and once the soil has warmed up. Plant on mounds of soil to ensure there is good drainage away from the base of the plant.

Mulch well to keep the soil moist. Put mulch or straw under developing fruit of pumpkins and other heavy winter squash to protect the skin while it is tender.

Tips

Mound-forming squash, with their tropical-looking leaves, can be added to borders as feature plants. Small-fruited trailing selections can be grown up trellises. The heavy-fruited trailing types will wind happily through a border of taller plants or shrubs. All squash can be grown in containers, though the mound-forming and shorter-trailing selections are usually most attractive; the long-trailing types end up as a stem that leads over the edge of the container.

Harvesting

Summer squash are tastiest when picked and eaten young. The more you pick, the more the plants will produce. Cut the fruit cleanly from the plant, and avoid damaging the leaves and stems to prevent disease and insect problems.

Winter squash should be harvested carefully, to avoid damaging the skins, just before the first hard frost. Allow them to cure in a warm, dry place for a few weeks until the skins become thick and hard. They can then be stored in a cool, dry place, where they should keep all winter.

Check them regularly to be sure they aren't spoiling.

Recommended

Squash plants are generally similar in appearance, with medium to large leaves held on long stems. Plants are trailing in habit, but some form only very short vines, so they appear to be more mound forming. Bright yellow, trumpet-shaped male and female flowers are borne separately but on the same plant. Female flowers can be distinguished by their short stems and by the juvenile fruit at the base

of the flower. Male flowers have longer stems.

C. pepo is the largest group of squash and includes summer squash, such as zucchini, and many winter squash, such as pumpkin, acorn squash, spaghetti squash, dumpling squash and gourds. Summer squash are ready to harvest in 45–50 days, and the winter squash in this group take from 70–75 days for acorn and spaghetti squash to 95–120 days for some of the larger pumpkins.

Problems & Pests

Problems with mildew, cucumber beetles, stem borers, bacterial wilt and whiteflies can occur. Ants may snack on damaged plants and fruit, and mice will eat and burrow into squash for the seeds in autumn.

Don't worry if some of your summer squash are too mature or your winter squash are not mature enough. Summer squash can be cured and will keep for a couple of months. They are still useful for baking into muffins and loaves. Immature winter squash can be harvested and used right away; try them stuffed, baked or barbequed.

Strawberry

Fragaria

Features: spreading perennial; soft, bright green leaves; white, sometimes pink flowers; bright red, edible fruit **Height:** 15–30 cm (6–12") **Spread:** 30 cm (12") or more **Hardiness:** zones 3–8

Many of these plants, with their pretty little flowers, spread vigorously by runners. Long shoots spread out from the parent plant, and small baby plants grow at the tips. Purchasing just a few plants will quickly provide you with plenty of fruit-producing plants by the end of summer.

Growing

Strawberries grow well in **full sun** or **light shade**. The soil should be **fertile, neutral to alkaline, moist** and **well drained**. These plants tolerate acidic soil but don't produce as much fruit.

Some selections can be started indoors about 12 weeks before you

plan to plant them outside. Other selections are only available as crowns or plants. Plant them outdoors around the last frost date. They tolerate light frosts.

Tips

Strawberries make interesting, tasty, quick-growing groundcovers. They do well in containers, window boxes and hanging baskets. The selections that don't produce runners are also good for edging beds.

Harvesting

Pick strawberries as soon as they are ripe. Some types produce a single large crop of fruit in early summer, and others produce a smaller crop throughout most or all of summer.

Recommended

F. chiloensis (Chilean strawberry), *F. vesca* (wild strawberry, alpine strawberry) and *F. virginiana* (Virginia strawberry) have been crossed to form many hybrids. Similar in appearance, they generally form a low clump of three-part leaves and

may or may not produce runners. Flowers in spring are followed by early- to midsummer fruit. Some plants produce a second crop in autumn, and others produce fruit all summer. The fruit of wild or alpine strawberries is smaller than the fruit of the other two species. Popular cultivars include mid-season producers **'Cabot'** and **'Kent'** and everbearing producers **'Sweetheart,'** **'Temptation'** and **'Tristar.'**

Problems & Pests

The fruit is susceptible to fungal diseases, so a mulch is recommended to protect it. Plants are fairly problem free, though some leaf spot, spider mite and wilt problems can occur.

The name strawberry has an uncertain origin, perhaps originally being "strayberry" or "strewberry." It is certain, however, that the name has nothing to do with the practice of mulching the plants with straw to protect the fruit from dirt and fungal diseases.

Sumac

Rhus

Features: bushy, suckering, colony-forming, deciduous shrub; summer and autumn foliage; summer flowers; late-summer to autumn fruit **Height:** 60 cm–9 m (2–30') **Spread:** equal to or greater than height **Hardiness:** zones 3–9

Sumacs are undervalued and very useful in tough, rocky, dry planting sites where maintenance is unwelcome or very difficult. Because some are coarse textured, plant them where close-up aesthetics are not an issue. Because of their suckering habit, make sure they have a lot of room and can be left to their own devices.

Growing

Sumacs develop the best autumn colour in **full sun** but tolerate partial shade. The soil should be of **average fertility, moist** and **well drained**. Once established, sumacs can tolerate drought. Both male and female plants are needed for fruit to form.

These plants can become invasive. Remove suckers that come up where you don't want them. Cut out some of the oldest growth each year and allow some suckers to grow in to replace it. If the colony is growing in or near your lawn, you can mow down any young plants that pop up out of bounds.

Tips

Sumacs can be used to form a specimen group in a shrub or mixed border, in a woodland garden or on a sloping bank.

R. typhina 'Dissecta'

When pulling up suckers, be sure to wear gloves to avoid getting the unusual, onion-like odour all over your hands.

Harvesting

The clusters of fuzzy, red sumac fruits can be picked in autumn and steeped in cold water overnight. Strain and sweeten to taste to make a tart, pink beverage.

Recommended

R. aromatica (fragrant sumac) forms a low mound of suckering stems 60 cm–1.8 m (2–6') tall and 1.5–3 m (5–10') wide. This species tolerates hot, dry, exposed conditions. It can be used to prevent erosion on hills too steep for mowing. The foliage turns red or purple in autumn. **'Green Globe'** is a dense, rounded cultivar that grows about 1.8 m (6') tall, with an equal spread. **'Grow-Low'** ('Gro-low') is a groundcover growing about 60 cm (2') tall and spreading up to 2.4 m (8'). It grows well in full burning sun and under trees where medium light is available. However, the good autumn colour is sacrificed with lower light levels.

R. typhina 'Dissecta'

R. chinensis (Chinese sumac, nutgall tree) forms a suckering, upright small tree or large shrub. It grows 6–7.5 m (20–25') tall and spreads 4.5–7.5 m (15–25'). The bright green leaves turn yellow, orange or red in autumn. It bears yellowish white flowers in late summer and early autumn; fuzzy fruit ripens to orange or red in mid-autumn. **'September Beauty'** bears large flower clusters and has more dependably attractive autumn colour. It closely resembles the Japanese tree lilac but blooms in August rather than late spring. (Zones 5–8)

R. aromatica 'Dissecta'

R. copallina (flameleaf sumac, shining sumac, dwarf sumac) is a dense, compact grower when young but becomes more open and irregular as it matures. It grows 6–9 m (20–30') tall with an equal spread. The dark green, glossy leaves turn vivid shades of red in autumn. It bears clusters of creamy flowers in mid- to late summer, followed by fuzzy, red fruit in autumn. It tolerates dry and rocky situations but can spread rampantly, making it a poor choice for a small garden. PRAIRIE FLAME ('Morton') is a slow-growing dwarf cultivar. It grows about 1.2 m (4') tall and spreads 1.2–1.8 m (4–6'). The leaves turn brilliant red in autumn. (Zones 4–9)

R. glabra (smooth sumac) is a native shrub that forms a bushy, suckering colony. It grows 3–4.5 m (10–15') tall with an equal or greater spread.

R. typhina 'Dissecta' (above)
R. glabra (below)

Green, summer flower spikes are followed, on female plants, by the typical fuzzy, red fruit. The foliage turns brilliant shades of orange, red and purple in autumn. (Zones 3–8)

R. typhina (*R. hirta*; staghorn sumac) is a colony-forming, suckering shrub whose branches are covered with velvety fuzz. It grows 4.5–7.5 m (15–25') tall and spreads 7.5 m (25') or more. Fuzzy, yellow flowers are followed by hairy, red fruit. **'Dissecta'** has finely cut leaves that give the plant a lacy, graceful appearance. This cultivar is more compact than the species, growing 1.8 m (6') tall and spreading 3 m (10'). (Zones 3–8)

Problems & Pests
Blister, canker, caterpillars, dieback, leaf spot, powdery mildew, scale insects, wood rot and *Verticillium* wilt can afflict sumacs.

R. typhina

Sumacs well deserve their antler analogies. Especially in winter, the many angular, forked branches do look like the antlers of a majestic stag.

R. typhina

Walnut

Juglans

Features: ornamental tree; attractive aromatic foliage; inconspicuous flowers; yellow-green male catkins; nutritious, oily nuts encased in a pulpy husk **Height:** 12–30 m (40–100') **Spread:** 9–25 m (30–80') **Hardiness:** zones 5–8

Walnuts grow in East Asia, the Middle East, the Mediterranean and North and South America. Walnut was one of the many nut trees European settlers brought with them to Canada. The wood is prized for fine furniture making, and the nuts are used as food and a source of trendy salad oil. Years of hybridization have produced hardy, easier-to-shell nuts with good yields.

Growing

Walnuts prefer **full sun** in a **sheltered** area. The soil should be **deep** and **fertile**. As with all nut trees, walnuts should be planted when they are dormant. Select two- to three-year-old nursery stock; anything older will be difficult to transplant. Avoid damaging the taproot. Stake the tree and water deeply throughout the growing season for the first year.

Tips

It's best to plant nut trees away from apple trees or rhododendrons and azaleas. Nuts can have a detrimental effect on these plants. Also avoid planting black walnuts near vegetables for the same reason.

Do not add fallen walnut leaves to compost because they are toxic.

Harvesting

Once a week during the harvest season, place a sheet under the tree and give the limbs a good shake. A one- to two-month ripening season is common for most species. When fully ripe, Persian walnuts are fairly easy to hull. The robust shells of black walnuts and butternuts will require considerably more muscle. Use a hammer or, for large amounts, try driving over them with the car!

Recommended

J. ailanthifolia var. *cordiformis* (heart nut) hails from Japan and seldom grows larger than an apple tree, which can be an advantage for the average garden. Its tendency to be low growing and spreading, however, does require some effort to encourage the tree to stretch up rather than out. Prune off a few of the lower limbs each year and cut back the longer laterals. New growth that competes with the leader should also be cut back. The heart-shaped nuts are mild, with a taste similar to pine nuts, grow in clusters like grapes and are not as prolific as Persian or black walnuts.

J. cinerea (butternut, white walnut) has a delicate root system and is often grafted to vigorous walnut rootstocks. The nuts are exceptionally tasty and may be soaked in water for several hours to make them easy to crack. Try **'Beckwith,' 'George Elmer'** or **'Kenworthy.'**

J. cinerea

J. x *bixbyi* (buartnut), as the common name suggests, is a cross between butternut and heartnut. One of the largest walnuts, it can have a metre-plus trunk diameter and grow 12 m (40') tall with a 25 m (80') crown. It is fast growing, reaching 1.8 m (6') in two years, and will bear in four to six years. **'Mitchell'** is a disease resistant, vigorous variety developed in Ontario.

J. nigra (black walnut) can grow up to 30 m (100' tall). **'Franquette'** is self-pollinating and late-blooming, an advantage in frosty areas. Thin-shelled **'Thomas'** bears on the young tree and continues with abundant harvests.

J. regia (Persian walnut, English walnut) is an excellent nut tree, producing flavourful, thin-shelled nuts. Carpathian types are the hardiest, with nuts ripening in a comparatively short season in late September, but they tend to leaf-out early and may be damaged by late-spring frosts. **'Wilson's Wonder'** fruits at around seven years as opposed to the usual 12-year wait.

J. regia

Problems & Pests

You might encounter leaf spot, walnut anthracnose or insect larvae infestation. Squirrels can also be a problem. Butternut suffers from blight, scale and fungus.

Walnuts are versatile trees, providing shade and ornament for the garden and valuable timber and veneers for furniture. The nuts can be harvested for food, used as a fabric dye or used as a source for sepia-type ink.

J. nigra 'Dissecta' (above & below)

Watermelon
Citrullus

Features: climbing or trailing vine; yellow flowers; decorative, edible fruit **Height:** 30 cm (12") **Spread:** 1.5–3 m (5–10') **Hardiness:** annual

Tasty and juicy, watermelon is the ultimate summer treat. It grows best in hot, humid weather, but plenty of short-season varieties are available for Canadian gardeners.

Growing

Watermelon grows best in **full sun**. The soil should be **fertile, humus rich, moist** and **well drained**. This plant likes plenty of water during the growth and early fruiting stages but, to intensify the flavour, should be allowed to dry out a bit once the fruit is ripening.

Watermelon requires a long growing season and should be started indoors four to six weeks early in individual peat pots. Started plants can also be purchased at garden centres and nurseries. Transplant them into the garden after the last frost date and once the soil has warmed up.

Tips

Small-fruited watermelon makes an attractive climbing specimen for patio containers, though even the small fruit may need some support as it grows. This plant can be left to wind through ornamental beds and borders.

Harvesting

A watermelon is generally ready to pick when the pale white area on the skin where the fruit sits turns yellow. Some experimentation may be required before you become adept at judging the ripeness of the fruit.

Recommended

C. lanatus is a trailing vine that takes 65–105 days to mature. The fruit skin may be light green with dark green stripes or solid dark green. The flesh may be red, pink, orange or yellow. Popular early-maturing cultivars include '**Gypsy,**' '**New Queen,**' '**Sugar Baby**' and '**Yellow Doll.**'

Problems & Pests

Problems with powdery mildew, *Fusarium* wilt, cucumber beetles and sap beetles can occur. Watermelon fruit blotch is a serious problem that can affect this plant, but it has not been found in Canada.

Wintergreen
Teaberry
Gaultheria

Features: glossy, dark green, wintergreen-scented foliage; white or pale pink, urn-shaped, summer flowers; persistent, aromatic, red fruit **Height:** 15–20 cm (6–8") **Spread:** 60–90 cm (24–36") **Hardiness:** zones 3–8

*T*his woodlander is a pretty, fragrant plant native to eastern North America and is worth growing for the glossy foliage that contrasts nicely with the persistent, red fruit. It also makes a wonderful terrarium plant, but be sure to buy nursery-grown plants rather than dig them from the woods.

Growing

Wintergreen grows best in **light shade** or **partial shade**, though it may tolerate full sun in consistently moist soil. The soil should be of **average fertility, neutral to acidic, peaty** and **moist**.

Tips

These lovely plants are at home in a moist woodland garden and can be included in a shaded border.

Harvesting

Both the leaves and berries are useful flavouring agents. The leaves can be harvested at any time; the berries can be harvested as soon as they turn bright red. Be aware, some people are allergic to wintergreen.

Recommended

G. procumbens is a low, spreading plant with glossy, dark green leaves that smell of wintergreen when crushed. White or pale pink, urn-shaped flowers are produced in summer and are followed by fragrant, red berries that persist through winter.

Problems & Pests

As with most herbs, wintergreen is relatively pest-free.

Wintergreen has a long history of herbal and medicinal use. The leaves are used for tea that is reputed to aid in breathing. The fruit is edible and has a distinctive flavour. The oil was used as a flavouring in toothpaste and root beer, but the flavour has been duplicated and is now produced synthetically.

TREE HEIGHT LEGEND: Short: < 25' (7. 5 m) • Medium: 25–50' (7.5–15 m) • Tall: > 50' (15 m)

SPECIES by Common Name	FORM								FOLIAGE						
	Tall Tree	Med. Tree	Short Tree	Shrub	Vine	Perennial	Annual		Evergreen	Deciduous	Variegated	Green	Yellow/Orange	Purple/Red	Blue/White
Almond • Apricot		•								•		•			
Apple	•	•	•							•		•			
Banana						•						•			•
Bayberry			•						•	•		•			
Beech	•									•		•	•	•	
Blueberry • Cranberry • Huckleberry				•					•	•		•	•	•	
Cape Gooseberry					•		•					•			
Cherry	•	•	•	•						•		•	•	•	
Chestnut	•	•	•	•						•		•			
Chokeberry				•						•		•		•	
Citrus			•	•					•			•			
Currant • Gooseberry				•						•		•			
Elderberry				•						•		•	•		
Fig		•	•							•		•			
Ginkgo	•	•								•		•	•		
Goji Berry				•						•		•			
Grape					•	•				•		•			
Hawthorn		•								•		•		•	
Hazelnut			•	•						•		•			
Highbush Cranberry				•					•	•		•		•	
Juniper Berry			•	•					•			•			•
Kiwi					•	•				•	•	•		•	•
Melon					•		•					•			
Mulberry		•	•	•						•		•	•		
Olive		•							•			•			
Oregon Grapeholly				•					•			•		•	
Passionfruit					•	•						•			
Peach • Nectarine			•							•		•			
Peanut							•					•			

FLOWERS						FRUIT		HARDINESS				SPECIES by Common Name
Red/Pink	Yellow/Orange	Green	Purple/Blue	White	Inconspicuous	Summer	Autumn	Hardy	Semi-hardy	Tender	Page Number	
•			•			•			•		84	Almond • Apricot
•		•	•			•	•	•	•		86	Apple
	•		•			•	•			•	90	Banana
					•		•	•	•		92	Bayberry
					•		•			•	94	Beech
•			•			•	•	•	•		96	Blueberry • Cranberry • Huckleberry
	•		•	•			•			•	100	Cape Gooseberry
•			•			•	•	•	•		102	Cherry
			•				•		•		106	Chestnut
			•				•	•	•		108	Chokeberry
			•			•	•			•	110	Citrus
•	•			•		•		•	•		114	Currant • Gooseberry
			•				•	•	•		118	Elderberry
		•			•	•	•		•	•	120	Fig
	•			•		•	•	•	•		122	Ginkgo
		•	•				•		•		124	Goji Berry
	•		•	•		•	•	•	•		126	Grape
•			•				•	•	•		130	Hawthorn
					•		•	•	•		134	Hazelnut
			•				•	•	•		136	Highbush Cranberry
					•			•	•		138	Juniper Berry
			•			•	•	•	•		140	Kiwi
	•					•				•	142	Melon
		•	•	•		•			•		146	Mulberry
			•				•			•	148	Olive
	•					•	•		•		150	Oregon Grapeholly
			•	•		•	•		•	•	152	Passionfruit
•						•	•		•		154	Peach • Nectarine
	•						•		•	•	158	Peanut

TREE HEIGHT LEGEND: Short: < 25' (7. 5 m) • Medium: 25–50' (7.5–15 m) • Tall: > 50' (15 m)

SPECIES by Common Name	FORM								FOLIAGE						
	Tall Tree	Med. Tree	Short Tree	Shrub	Vine	Perennial	Annual		Evergreen	Deciduous	Variegated	Green	Yellow/Orange	Purple/Red	Blue/White
Pear	•	•	•							•		•	•	•	•
Pecan • Hickory	•									•		•	•		
Persimmon		•								•		•			
Pine Nut	•	•	•	•					•			•			
Pineapple						•						•	•		
Plum		•	•	•						•		•		•	
Prickly Pear						•			•			•		•	•
Quince		•								•		•	•		
Raspberry • Blackberry				•						•		•			
Rhubarb						•						•		•	
Rosehip				•						•		•			
Serviceberry		•	•	•						•		•	•	•	
Squash					•		•					•			
Strawberry						•						•			
Sumac		•	•	•						•		•	•	•	
Walnut	•									•		•			
Watermelon					•		•					•			
Wintergreen						•						•			

SPECIES
by Common Name

Red/Pink	Yellow/Orange	Green	Purple/Blue	White	Inconspicuous	Summer	Autumn	Hardy	Semi-hardy	Tender	Page Number	Species
•				•			•		•		160	Pear
					•		•		•		164	Pecan • Hickory
				•			•		•		166	Persimmon
				•		•	•	•	•		168	Pine Nut
•		•								•	172	Pineapple
•				•		•	•	•	•		174	Plum
•	•			•			•		•	•	180	Prickly Pear
•				•			•		•		182	Quince
•				•		•	•	•	•		184	Raspberry • Blackberry
•	•	•				•		•	•		188	Rhubarb
•			•	•			•	•	•		190	Rosehip
				•		•		•	•		192	Serviceberry
	•					•	•		•		196	Squash
•				•		•	•	•	•		200	Strawberry
	•	•		•		•	•	•	•		202	Sumac
					•		•		•		206	Walnut
	•					•				•	210	Watermelon
•				•			•	•	•		212	Wintergreen

GLOSSARY

annual: a plant that germinates, flowers, sets seed and dies in one growing season

B&B: abbreviation for balled-and-burlapped stock, i.e., plants that have been dug out of the ground and have had their root balls wrapped in burlap

bonsai: the art of training plants into minature trees and landscapes

candles: the new, soft spring growth of needle-leaved evergreens such as pine

crown: the part of a plant at or just below the soil where the stems meet the roots; also, the top of a tree, including the branches and leaves

cultivar: a cultivated plant variety with one or more distinct differences from the species; e.g., in flower colour, leaf variegation or disease resistance

damping off: a fungal disease causing seedlings to rot at soil level and topple over

deadhead: to remove spent flowers to maintain a neat appearance and encourage a longer blooming period

dieback: death of a branch from the tip inward; usually used to describe winter damage

direct sow: to sow seeds directly in the garden where plants are to grow, as opposed to sowing first in pots or flats for transplanting

disbud: to remove some flowerbuds to improve the size or quality of the remaining ones

dormancy: an inactive stage, often coinciding with the onset of winter

dripline: the area around the bottom of a tree, directly under the tips of the farthest-extending branches

dwarf: a plant that is small compared to the normal growth of the species; dwarf growth is often cultivated

espalier: the training of a tree or shrub to grow in two dimensions

forma (f.): a naturally occurring variant of a species; below the level of subspecies and similar to variety

gall: an abnormal outgrowth or swelling produced as a reaction to sucking insects, other pests or diseases

genus: a category of biological classification between the species and family levels; the first word in a scientific name indicates the genus

girdling: the restricted flow of water and nutrients in a plant caused by something tied tightly around a trunk or branch, or by an encircling cut or root

grafting: a type of propagation in which a stem or bud of one plant is joined onto the rootstock of another plant of a closely related species

habit: the growth form of a plant, comprising its size, shape, texture and orientation

harden off: to gradually acclimatize plants that have been growing in a protective environment to a more harsh environment

hardy: capable of surviving unfavourable conditions, such as cold or frost, without protection

hip: the fruit of a rose, containing the seeds

humus: decomposed or decomposing organic material in the soil

hybrid: any plant that results from natural or human-induced cross-breeding between varieties, species or genera; hybrids are often sterile but may be more vigorous than either parent and have attributes of both

leader: the dominant upward growth at the top of a tree; may be erect or drooping

node: the area on a stem from where leaves grow

offset: a horizontal branch that forms at the base of a plant and produces new plants from buds at its tips

perennial: a plant that takes three or more years to complete its life cycle; a herbaceous perennial normally dies back to the ground over winter

pH: a measure of acidity or alkalinity (the lower the pH below 7, the greater the acidity; the higher the pH between 7 and 14, the greater the alkalinity); soil pH influences nutrient availability for plants

pollarding: a severe form of pruning in which all younger branches of a tree are cut back virtually to the trunk to encourage bushy new growth

rhizome: a modified stem that grows horizontally underground

root ball: the root mass and surrounding soil of a container-grown or dug-out plant

runner: a modified stem that grows on the soil surface; roots and new shoots are produced at nodes along its length

semi-evergreen: evergreen plants that in cold climates lose some or all of their leaves over winter

semi-hardy: a plant capable of surviving the climatic conditions of a given region if protected from heavy frost or cold

species: the original plant from which cultivars are derived; the fundamental unit of biological classification, indicated by a two-part scientific name, e.g., *Pinus mugo* (*mugo* is the specific epithet)

standard: a shrub or small tree grown with an erect main stem; accomplished either through pruning and training or by grafting the plant onto a tall, straight stock

subspecies (subsp.): a naturally occurring, regional form of a species, often geographically isolated from other subspecies but still potentially able to inter-breed with them

sucker: a shoot that comes up from a root, often some distance from the plant; it can be separated to form a new plant once it develops its own roots

tender: incapable of surviving the climatic conditions of a given region and requiring protection from frost and cold

true: the passing of desirable characteristics from the parent plant to seed-grown offspring; also called breeding true to type

variegation: describes foliage that has more than one colour, often patched or striped or bearing differently coloured leaf margins

variety (var.): a naturally occurring variant of a species; below the level of subspecies in biological classification

INDEX

About the Authors

Louise Donnelly is the former garden and cookbook columnist for *BC BookWorld* and continues there as a contributing editor. For many years she worked for an Okanagan Valley orchard fruit market as an in-house writer and book buyer. She lives in a log house on a small acreage that was once part of the historic BX Ranch and, as a keen but amateur backyard gardener, is delighted when the raspberries are ripe.

Alison Beck has been gardening since she was a child. Author of more than two dozen gardening books, she showcases her talent for practical advice and her passion for gardening. Alison has a diploma in Horticultural Technology and a degree in Creative Writing.